PHILIPPINES

HÉLÈNE CIXOUS

TRANSLATED BY LAURENT MILESI

polity

First published in French as *Philippines: Prédelles* © Éditions Galilée, 2009

This English edition © Polity Press, 2011

This text was first read in the original on the occasion of the International Symposium 'Hélène Cixous. Croire rêver. Arts de penser', which was held at the Cité internationale universitaire, Maison Henirich Heine, Fondation de l'Allemagne, from 16 to 18 June 2008, organized by Bruno Clément (Collège international de philosophie) and Marta Segarra (Centro Dona i Literatura, University of Barcelona). A prior, shorter version was given as a keynote lecture at the University of Sussex in early June 2008, the first part of which was subsequently published as 'Philippines. Sweet Prison', trans. Laurent Milesi, *Oxford Literary Review*, vol. 30, no. 2: 'Telepathies', ed. Nicholas Royle (2008), pp. 257–81.

Polity Press
65 Bridge Street
Cambridge CB2 1UR, UK

Polity Press
350 Main Street
Malden, MA 02148, USA

ISBN-13: 978-0-7456-4815-6
ISBN-13: 978-0-7456-4816-3(pb)

A catalogue record for this book is available from the British Library.

Typeset in 11.5 on 15 pt Janson Text
by Servis Filmsetting Ltd, Stockport, Cheshire
Printed and bound in Great Britain by MPG Books Group Limited,
Bodmin, Cornwall

For further information on Polity, visit our website: www.politybooks.com

CONTENTS

ACKNOWLEDGEMENTS

"Mandorla" from *Poems of Paul Celan*, translated by Michael Hamburger. Translation copyright © 1972, 1980, 1988, 2002 by Michael Hamburger. Reprinted by permission of Persea Books, Inc., New York.

AUTHOR'S NOTE

Let's return to the starting point.
Every one of us has a secret book. It is a cherished book. It is not beautiful. Not great. Not so well written. We don't care. For it is goodness itself for us. The absolute friend. It promises and lives up to what it promises. We forget it but it never forgets us. It knows everything about us but it does not know it knows. If Freud had been asked to name his secret(ive) book, he would not have hesitated: it would have been *The Jungle Book*. The one book Proust loved above all others was *Le Capitaine Fracasse*. Proust might have read the book which makes me weep. I myself never read it: I dream it. I live it again. This book about which you see me thinking, as if I could see its two characters, sitting in the corner of the hall, gently holding hands, this book with almost supernatural powers, no doubt its title will seem as foreign to

you as the character of the Capitaine Fracasse is to me, its loud-sounding name: *Peter Ibbetson*. I hold it as dear as the apple of my eye, just as I hold dear the condition, the law, the grace, of my whole life: *the gift of dreaming true, through the prison bars*. Isn't this book some sort of fortune-telling book for me? I never think about it.

This Peter has a twin sister. She is Gradiva. The two books were born at a distance and at the same time, each in a different language. Perhaps from an undiagnosed telepathy?

They tell the same story. It is about death and resurrection. The author? now he is called George du Maurier, now he is called Wilhelm Jensen. The author has a similar stroke of genius. This stroke of genius is so strong that it can take place only once. Genius is stronger than the author. Same for the Apocalypse. The illumination takes place only once. So that it can be said that there is no author any longer. *The Book of Revelation is dictated by a telepathic act*. 'The author' will have been the medium for a manifestation of supernatural forces. The two authors in question are true conductors of these thunderstriking phenomena. The whole irradiating truth is gathered in the destiny of one single soul with two bodies: Peter and his Tower, the Duchess of Towers. Look. From one second to the next, our heroes are hurled forever *into the same psychical space*. What takes place? During the initial collision, there is a transference of the seat of life to the place of the other. This can be compared to a *postnatal twinship*. Each makes the life of the other. The first who dies kills the other by telepathy.

Peter Ibbetson says something to me

Is it a book? What is a book? What am I doing when I

lock myself with it in a feverish tête-à-tête from which I cannot wrench myself? I get up ten times. I return to the book, I am summoned, bewitched, held back by the mysterious forces of Reading. I can hear its siren's murmur: *Let's return to the starting point*, come on, come with me. And that's what I want above all: I want a book to make itself dream [*fasse rêve*] and bring me back to childhoods. To read is nothing but that, is it not? To return to oneself in prehistory, in those legendary times when we were toddling and telepathing round the world on all fours and eight paws to see where its opening was. As always for those expeditions, the traveller must be able to have at his disposal in the book these magic primitive objects which will enable him to establish radio links with legendary times. Starting for me with: *a Gate*.

And also: *a Garden*. One keeping (watch over) the other. There is a child. We are in his timeless gaze.

When one day I find out, when I recognize my garden, I will ask myself how Peter Ibbetson's garden at Auteuil could have been, from a distance in time and in space, the dazzling prefigure of the Garden of the Cercle Militaire in Oran.

Peter Ibbetson, you say. Which one? The book? The film? Or else the prisoner or the escapee? For there are two *Peter Ibbetson*s which make philippine from a distance, one being the one who dreams, the other the one who is dreamt, one returning from the other, to the other. It so happens that *Peter Ibbetson* the first, the one who brought me to tears, with which I first found myself behind bars, will have been the film *Peter Ibbetson*.

It was the most beautiful film in the world.

This film by Henry Hathaway was not a film, I want

to make it clear. It's a Revelation. The true authors of this Dream filmed in a state of dream are the adorable Inventors of the *Dreaming True*, the Great Dreamed Ones whose names are sometimes Peter and Mary, but not always. Like all those invited in dreams, they have transfigureal names and figures: sometimes Gogo, Mimsey, Gary Cooper, they are themselves mistaken, fail to know themselves, tremble with emotion, which allows them to taste the painful happiness of double love. Of dual love. Under the borrowed names, under the new bodies which lead them astray, under the foliage whose French look conceals the fabulous forest of *A Midsummer Night's Dream*, they are subjected to the laws of a strange attraction. The everlasting childhood which plays within them on the ruins of names thwarts the Prisons and Towers of lost time . . .

It is time I returned to my subject, which is *Philippine*. Or Philippines.

Now I am going to tell you the secret of *Philippine*: it's an *amande* with an *a*. It's an almond with two almonds. One of the two almonds has to make amends. It follows that the other also has to amend. It's a play of almonds. A double play. What is there in *Amande*? There is the double charm of an *âme* (soul) which sum*monds* two people not to forget each other, to call each other by the same name, to precede each other, to echo, dissociate and reflect each other. As if they were mutually almonding and amending each other.

From almond to almond the almond enshrines itself, promises itself, steals away, receives, an emblematic fruit of hospitality, *Mandorla* for the Virgin with child, host and hostess, passive and active, chaste and destined to be peeled, as I am doing now by opening the envelope of its names. Philippine is the androgynous almond. It always thinks about love.

Let's return to the gate of the first garden: we are always on *the other side* of bars. Look on the other side. You see?

Let's return – *revenons*.

Days of a neat, pure and ruling sun, moments when one truly sees all the realities, starting with the muddled hearts of men and the burning arena of the first wars and the extraordinary beauty of trees that watch human carnage, a novelty, and the voiceless pain of the skinned calf. These days have an unforgettable address (rue Philippe).

'*Revenons*' will be my first word. As long as I shall live, and even more perhaps.

Let's return to our starting point [Revenons à notre point de départ].

As soon as I hear this word, this sentence, *revenons*, I feel uplifted by a melancholy enthusiasm. Warm winds hailing from the word – rather than the trains which whistle for Proust – and I have already yielded to the temptation to

I shall sing of the infinite mighty power of such a sentence, for me, over me, in me. Of the quasi-omnipotence – for instance, of this one: *Revenons à notre point de départ.* You're disappointed? Maybe it seems ordinary to you, dull as a lead casket? And yet. I've got another one for you, which is apparently more seductive, culled in the dawn of this spring morning.

Hold your crown tight [tiens ferme ta couronne]. *I feel I have in my mind like the Lake of Geneva invisible at night.* I have the faces of four young girls, two bell towers,

1

a noble lineage, a 'let's go further' in the Normandy hydrangea, which I don't know what I will do with <sometimes become fetishes whose meaning I no longer know [. . .]¹

'Hold your crown tight. I feel I have in my mind like the Lake of Geneva invisible at night.' I read this and I weep. Tears, tears of joy. Tears at being reunited. Reunited with my lost paradise. I weep over learning, as I find it again, that I had lost it, I weep over finding it again in order to lose it. I weep with the joy of weeping. As long as I weep, it is still here, enduringly, sparkling under the fine shower of tears I hold my crown with a passionate shudder. Its circle contains as many treasures as a magic cup of tea. I have here the first fragrant essences of the earth, a red earth where worms of a live-red glass squirm, Mamma's forceful absence, my tiny little brother squatting in a corner, a vast military storm over my heads, soon there will be jeeps, tanks, helicopters and a handful of overblonde children, oh yes and a big stone too, a temple for an anthill which is the whole of humankind. The perimeter is made up of tall stalks of a golden metal. Gate [*grille*]. And sentences burning like red pimiento spat out by a viper's tongue on that face of mine with its forever lost smile. At age three this child already knows everything that is in store for her. The times are near. Death enters. Already! And a 'let's return to our starting point' which startles me with a violent prophetic happiness, which becomes that very instant a fetish whose meaning I do not know, which picks me up and saves me. Which brings me back home, with tears which necessity changes into an intense reflexion. Hold, shut your crown tight

2

[*tiens, ferme ta couronne*], I say to myself keeping for later all those pieces that shine true.

That was on 21 March. In 2008.

I had just *found*. Cobblestones trodden with joy. A sentence of gold and silver which glistens on the cobblestones of rue du Cercle Militaire. It is mine since I found it. I apply the literary principle here. Just as Proust finds his magic crown in a wood of Nerval's. He takes it. And becomes a daughter of fire. Another time, not far from a track beaten by Chateaubriand, there he becomes a 'realized sylph'. I apply the alchemy of literary telepathy here, whose formula, well known to the fanatics, is: '*Senancour c'est moi*' (Senancour: that's me). In a single word, just as '*ces âmes*' (these souls) sounds like '*sésame*' (sesame): *Senancourcémoi*. Among dreamers of the true there is communication. A banal and marvellous phenomenon. One walks in the forests of books and suddenly this is my crown, it is the very sensation. Here's a sentence wholly my own: 'Which proves a mysterious relation between – (truth and natural beauty, X's brain and H's heart).'

I live on the hypothesis that there would have been one single huge Garden from the beginning of time whose circle-shaped enclosure would hold a set G of gardens which have whirled about since time immemorial and alight here and there in the instant of a foreign garden.

'Hold your crown tight [*Tiens ferme ta couronne*]' . . .

Did I write this sentence? I must have written it in another life. Or else dreamt it. And returned [*revenue*]. I recognize it from the happiness which it kindles in me and which awakens me.

Let's return to our starting point. (Which starting point? where? who? what?) Don't leave. 'To-day we will proceed along a narrow, uneven path, but one which will lead us to a magnificent prospect.' Pretend it is Dr Freud who's telling you this and lend a benevolent ear to what I'm going to say. Since I have lived with this sentence (*Revenons*, etc.) for a month, I know its force and that under its modest appearance it is charged with desires, with promises of incredible delights, and with magic nostalgias. It does not sound like much but deliberately so. In truth it knows everything. Out of tenderness and politeness it presents itself like an effortless, slightly vague, yet pressing invitation. You remember this extravagant path which Proust took in order to initiate us into the mysteries of 'the instigatrix whose magic keys unlock at the bottom of ourselves the door of abodes into which we would not have known how to step', that is to say, *La Lecture* (Reading), also called 'the original psychological act'? You remember that, in order to lead us to think what Reading is, he proceeded to evoke in minute detail the places and days when he himself made the discovery of the Original Act, and how he guided us in his Reading Chamber, a real bazaar or else a supernatural and familiar theatre whose stage is surrounded by several circles of curtains cut from different fabrics, in marceline, in cambric, in guipure, all of them white naturally.

How he made us enter and exit the sanctuary in order to lead us to another sanctuary, designed like the vegetal double of the inner chamber, an arbour shrouded in pruned hazelnut trees and located at the far end of the park, where the river ceases to be *a line of water covered with signs*, I mean *swans* [une ligne d'eau couverte de cygnes], and lined with statues, and like a book wings its way across the park enclosure.

You have not forgotten how this superposition of magic spells, a true grimoire full of signs . . .

is what he calls Reading.

You remember that this Itinerary leads us through space to the beginning of times, to the origin, to the first days of the creation of the prophetic soul, to the creator's childhood, before creation, to the state of the young Siddhartha under the boughs of his baobab.

You have not forgotten that, like a dreamer unsure as to whether he is being dreamt or awake, when, lagging behind, you felt you were lingering, through the suggestive force of a bard reincarnated from the legendary bards, 'along these flowery by-ways', it sometimes occurred to you to wonder where you were, in whose house, doing what, whereas you thought you could remember you had left in order to read, 'to read' a 'book', but to read, what is it? So a book was not what you thought it was, you had set out early in the morning, intent on reading a serious book by Proust, a solemn tome by Freud – and there we are in another book, and yet another, and then in a chamber full to the brim of the soul of others, there is *in the mandorla* Mamma's smiling face behind which I can hear a mocking bird's short burst of laughter, it's Papa, happy as a Holy Spirit, through the multicoloured panes of the glass door. I can see us, me and my brother, hiding under the sheets the secret life and all the secrets of the life lurking behind the curtain of the improvised theatre when we began inventing counter-stories, thus it means I have returned [*revenue*] *to 54 rue Philippe in Oran* while following in

5

young Proust's footsteps, at the dawn of creation, in the workshop of telepathies.

It's springtime. All of a sudden a need awakens, the ancient, ageless desire to drink the immortal songs of birds, birds die, songs resume, the need *to hear* invisible *Voices*, to watch the dead branches give way to the victorious buds, to set a limit to hibernation, and all those ancient forces which govern me, over me and in me, gather into a precise, shining, urgent idea: I want to read *Peter Ibbetson*. Read? Read the source, the torment, both together. Read? Appease the hunger of the soul which remembers the taste of illumination. Eat the light. Shed the tears. Restore the current of life cut off by winters. Set immortality in motion again. From a great distance, from the far end of the cave of secrets, Peter Ibbetson returns. I open the window. I hear his child's voices. Reading starts again! We were sick with death. The seed picks up again

> [. . .] during which the thousand sensations emanated from the depth of our good health follow the infinite movement of our thoughts and make up around it, from the flower of all our unconscious well-beings, the honey of a soft golden pleasure which mingles with our ardent meditation like a quiet smile. This art [. . .][2]

Books, deliver us, make us delirious [*livres, délivrez-nous, délirez-nous*], lead us into the garden of *Unland* where the flowers grow whose adored names we had forgotten, where, under the clumps of thyme perhaps or between the tall stalks of acanthus, I find the keys to the gates of immortality. A book is *something else* then? The real book, the one which has all the strengths of the inner fecundities, is that, the one which has the Power of Communication, which communicates this power to us while leaving our solitude intact

The miraculous book – which says to us: *let's return to the starting point*. This is the way I am going.

Each to their starting point. Each to their magic book. Each to their childhood and fatality.

How does communication take place?

Via 'telepathic *response*' I'd say. It's as if a book, which I do not know, which I believe I do not know, which I believe I do not ask anything from, personally, <u>*were only just responding to me*</u> while itself asking my own questions in front of me, in its language, whereas I said nothing, I say nothing, the story takes place in a foreign land, where I have never been, yet it is mine [*c'est le mien, c'est la mienne*], I don't return from it/I cannot believe it [*je n'en reviens pas*]. I believe it is him and yet it is me. It looks like a dream. Everything that happens to the characters which are not me, happens <u>in me</u>, to me, one day. It is not the events which strike me with astonishment, after all everybody falls, loves, dies, betrays, and deceives. What astounds me is the mental reservation [*arrière-pensée*], the murmur of sorrow and of indignation, the murmur of the thought behind the thought, the subtle, confidential air which circulates in the sentences. It is the sentences which gather the events, the choir, the song which interprets the destinies. And the signs, the details, all the signals each time unique through which a destiny translates itself into a reality. The setting for the action.

7

My signs: gates [*grilles*]; a stone, which seemed to me fairly big. A summer chirping. An infinite stretch of sand. A real garden. A Population of ficus populated with swifts. I'll add to this the desperate howl of a dog: I have forgotten this howl, it's my brother who remembers it. It often seems to me that I can hear my brother within me howling in the hole-filled garden, my brother-dog, my brother the dog. My desperate dog, the one that runs in me, has a mute howl. Where can this howl possibly be?

In prison. Everything is imprisoned. My dog is in prison, eternally in prison. In the end even its squeal is in prison. I too am in prison. In the crypt where I imprison myself, noises from the life outside no longer reach me. But there's my brother, that is to say, the foreign body, wholly outside of me, and which however is the familiar stone in my garden [*la pierre familière dans mon jardin*]. My brother Pierre too is in prison. He walks about with his prison on his back. I refrain from saying to him: 'Pierre, you cannot see this prison which you are carrying, it is too tight, it's a real corset, it makes you stiff.' My brother comes plodding in, lined with a wall. He sits down in the armchair, he lays down his burden. The armchair cracks. My brother cannot hear his dog squeal. My brother can hear my dog letting out the squeal I cannot hear. I can see my dog is nothing but a howl but it is my brother who hears it. My brother cannot hear himself, I am the one who does. I tell him a true dream. I saw. The dead person was alive and the living one dead.

– What does this mean? says my brother.

Now he wears glasses which are like portholes. We eventually decide to get used to them. – Some relations are totally unknown to us, says my brother. A sentence

8

wholly my own. Thereupon he tells me four stories which he presents as 'shaggy-dog incidents [*tirés par les cheveux*]'.

This is the name my brother gives to the incomprehensible facts which occur in his existence. Others would say telepathy. There are invisible threads. In the narrative each anecdote, once it is over, recalls another anecdote. My brother is extremely surprised. It is as if somebody he cannot see came behind him and pulled his leg [*le tirer par les cheveux*]. I don't say the word *telepathy* to my brother. I don't tell him that for a few weeks I've been playing with the chapters, in the works of Freud and of Jacques Derrida, whose fairy-like character is called Telepathy. I note these shaggy-dog stories [*histoires-tirées-par-les-cheveux*]. One of them is not so shaggy, he says. But still he likes it. I could tell them another time.

I listen to my brother. I call him inwardly. I don't call my brother by his name Pierre. Never. In my inner land I call him Pete. My brother recalls my dog which is also his dog, Fips the dog, without us being able to discover any explanation as to what brought him to this evocation at that very moment. There is no dog in the vicinity. It is the inner dog which woke up, no one knows how. I see him straightaway. He runs like mad in the Garden. He jumps over the totally impassable gates just as Remus jumps over the wall with which Romulus has just enclosed Rome. I'll never forget this scene. – Why did Fips set about howling his heart out [*hurler à la mort*] when Papa died? Twenty kilometres away he felt a soul was passing out? said my brother

My brother listens to Fips. – Nothing can be done about it, says my brother.

9

The sentence moans in all directions. Nothing can be done about death, about pain, about the strange tenacity of the immortal foreign body. 'Fips, I am dead,' says my father to his son the dog. It was Thursday 12 February 1948 at 11.45 am.

Telepathy is: without explanation.

Both of them linked at a distance in the same psychical garden, the same prison, shaken by the violent pity they feel for each other.

– What did you think? I say.

– Nothing. I remember he howled his heart out.

At that moment our father did not speak any longer. There was a transference of pain from one soul to the other.

The signs, the keys, the all-powerful accessories which command the genesis and decide, like the *ficus ruminalis*,[3] that here in a forgotten time the magic city of my birth was built, this construction of a prehistoric scene, as always for the keys, my signals are most commonplace in appearance. I cite them today: this does not mean that when they 'make an apparition' I recognize them immediately. On the contrary. I pass each time by those things so dear to me, sometimes I meet the object, an avenue of dragon trees which seems to lead to the entrance to the past, makes me jump, a rusty gate grates my heart, but no, time is too far, perhaps it is elsewhere, I cannot name the sensation, I remember there were tears but I no longer know who weeps – I feel as if I were going to my own unknown grave in a dream. The sensation tells me: name me. I do not know. It recedes sadly. Has not resurrected. Like Proust the day when, as he was crossing a pantry, a piece of green canvas blocking up a broken part of the glass pulled him up short. Halt! That's how it is: one passes in front of the curtain behind which stands the screen with the hole through which one must slip in order to get to the path that leads to the scene that knows. A summer radiance makes us pause. Stop! Listen. Do you hear? What? A summer beam [*rayonnement d'été*]. Why? From having been [*d'avoir été*]. Where? At the beginnings of Letherature.

I have never been here. It's even a town, a house a street where I'd avoid going. And yet I am here, find myself here, as if in me another who is me were staying here for me. And conversely: I am here at home, it's my home, my brain, my country my room and somebody else is living in it, true there are a few differences, thus the host may be a man, a sick person suffering from other illnesses than mine, the epoch does not matter for the inner time is like that of the dream . . . but for the rest, which is the main thing, fate is the same in the minutest details.

So there's a book that reads in my thoughts. One book or another. It's a fact. For some it can be a painting. It also happens to me, a painting reading in my thoughts.

– Do you believe in telepathy?
Don't respond. You have already responded.
What does Freud say?

You remember the *New Introductory Lectures to Psychoanalysis – Neue Folge der Vorlesungen zur Einführung in die Psychoanalyse* (these daughters or cousins of the *New Lectures on Psychoanalysis*, those that Freud wrote and

11

delivered in 1915–16 and 1916–17 – in the middle of the war, therefore with the war within himself as well), fantastic lectures born in his imagination in 1932, whose strange status he revealed to us in an overwhelming Preface:

> *Zum Unterschied hiervon sind diese neuen Vorlesungen niemals gehalten worden. Mein Alter hatte mich inzwischen der Verpflichtung enthoben, die – wenn auch nur peripherische – Zugehörigkeit zur Universität durch Abhaltung von Vorlesungen zum Ausdruck zu bringen, und eine chirurgische Operation hatte mich als Redner unmöglich gemacht. Es ist also nur eine Verspiegelung der Phantasie, wenn ich mich während der nachfolgenden Ausführungen wieder in den Hörsaal versetze; sie mag mithelfen, bei der Vertiefung in den Gegenstand die Rücksicht auf den Leser nicht zu vergessen.*

These new lectures, unlike the former ones, have never been delivered. My age had in the meantime absolved me from the obligation of giving expression to my membership of the University (which was in any case a peripheral one) by delivering lectures; and a surgical operation had made speaking in public impossible for me. If, therefore, I once more take my place in the lecture room during the remarks that follow, it is only by an artifice of the imagination; it may help me not to forget to bear the reader in mind as I enter more deeply into my subject.[4]

Thus only when talking (about them) has become forever impossible does he speak about them while resurrecting by magic a (lost) scene which never took place.

His body has become violently foreign to him. One will never know who in him surrenders to the charm of Telepathy.

I so much wish I had all the time to walk with the wounded old man along the narrow, sunken footpaths which lead in sight of the Promised Land. I don't have the time. Fortunately Jacques Derrida already took the first walk, that was in 1981, he called it 'Telepathy', thus giving this strange deity a proper, secretive name. *Telepathy* like Tarapatapoum, the fairy who saves child-hoods from the misfortunes which are in store for them.

Allow me, out of love for the noble female stranger, to beg you to reread all these texts which a carriage of telepathies sweeps along briskly up the hill and down the dale towards the lofty heights of philosophy, on this ridge from which the Magnificent View can be glimpsed. You will see enacted as in a shadow theatre the mock fight of the Titans, which does not oppose but confuses Freud and Derrida, riding [*roulant*] from one to the other, taking each other for a ride [*se roulant*], pulling each to himself all the faux bonds and the Protean lures, in order not to speak the Telepatruth [*Véritélépathie*] while speaking it. *They steal the show from each other.*

I resorted to my all-powerful friend the Dream. I was hiding in my arbour, at last, there was a deep silence. There was no time left, the risk of being found out was almost nil. I could hear Freud's voice droning out the first beats of his second imaginary lecture, the one enti-tled 'Dreams and Occultism', '*Traum und Okkultismus*', which has two number systems, *Lecture 2* and *Lecture 30* since it is propped up by the legs and paws [*s'appuie pour marcher sur les membres, les pattes*] of the one that came before. 'Ladies and Gentlemen,' he says, 'today we will proceed along a narrow path, etc.' All this was taking place in Freud's head on the one hand, in my head on the other hand. Freud could no longer speak, except in spirit. That was on 21 March 2008. 'The Surprise is what is waiting for us up there, when we have reached the top of the climb,' I said to my mother and to my daughter. I did not have an idea of the surprise, I had a certainty of it. But it is not easy to get there, for you have to drive the car as if it were a camel or a horse, on the mountain. The beast pants. True, at the beginning of the ascent, there is a thin road between the trees and the cliffs, enough space to creep in between the sharp bends. Even if one sees, looming farther up, a lorry that takes up the whole width of the path. One goes under the wheels one won't know how. Then there was no road anymore, at least this much was getting clearer it seems, for there was nothing but rocks, stones and scree, but I assured Ève that the car could still climb, good beast, it bent the paws of its rubber wheels, we still had a little to go when we reached the site where the workers were digging out what will perhaps be a passage or a tunnel. Tons of sand are being excavated, there was a frail roof of ballast, better push on as soon as possible for if that collapsed over us. We now cross the contractor's glass office, and at last we emerge on the roof of the world. None of us four thinks that this is another name for Tibet. The word remains in secret. What a surprise! An immense panorama unfolded its incredible landscapes in a dream of maximal dimension.

Landscapes are more forceful than souls, what makes me think of a dream is the aura which emanates softly like a summer radiance. The Town itself had unfurled, with its floods of houses, of temples with pointed roofs right and left depending on where I turned my eyes. Towards the west one surely would have seen the sea. The Town rose. The dream did not carry beyond The Town but I had no doubt. Over there it's the sea, it is in the indicative present, even if I cannot see it. A strong sense of *déjàvu* as in a dream crept over me. Sometimes even, I said to myself, on the inclined plane of the imperfects full of halftones, the indicative present performs a straightening up, I have alreadythought that, this is when, having passed the things that pass – it was the low-roofed house of the Clos-Salembier with a garden sleeping on the Algiers hill – a hazy light gives an aura to the more durable reality which keeps watch in dreams and awaits us, at the end of the sunken footpath up there, from where, always, the sea can be glimpsed. Then one is swamped by the inner flood of revelation, we are infused with light. All this is of an incredible beauty, nobody can doubt it, it is the True Beauty, that which one contemplates only within the dream, when we are ourselves at the top and within ourselves. I did tell you, I said, *this is what* (till now) *we had no knowledge of.*

And in order to climb back down, there is just this footpath which goes very fast to the familiar road. This is the way I came by chance yesterday, not knowing that, if one pushed further on, one would get to this monumental triumph. I guessed that such an exaltation could not be granted to just any passer-by. One must introduce oneself in one's genealogy, for there is an obvious relation between the expansion of space and the lengthening of time. I came with past and future in order to fulfil in reality Freud's prediction which inaugurates his new imaginary lectures: follow the Path (I note he mumbles the word *path* in English, that way: *Wir werden heute einen schmalen Weg gehen, let us follow the path* – the *pathy*, he had said – the narrow path of the *pathy* which leads to the discovery of the eternal mother). I know that you know – in regard to your own relations with people and things – *the meaning of the starting point.*

DIE ZERLEGUNG DER PSYCHISCHEN PERSÖNLICHKEIT

Meine Damen und Herren! Ich weiß, Sie kennen für Ihre eigenen Beziehungen, ob es sich um Personen oder um Dinge handelt, die Bedeutung des Ausgangspunktes. So war es auch mit der Psychoanalyse. Für die Entwicklung, die sie nahm, für die Aufnahme, die sie fand, ist es nicht gleichgültig gewesen, daß sie ihre Arbeit am Symptom begann, am Ichfremdesten, das sich in der Seele vorfindet. Das Symptom stammt vom Verdrängten ab, ist gleichsam der Vertreter desselben vor dem Ich, das Verdrängte ist aber für das Ich Ausland, inneres Ausland, so wie die Realität – gestatten Sie den ungewohnten Ausdruck – äußeres Ausland ist.

THE DISSECTION OF THE PSYCHICAL PERSONALITY

LADIES AND GENTLEMEN, – I know you are aware in regard to your own relations, whether with people or things, of the importance of your starting-point. This was also the case with psycho-analysis. It has not been a matter of indifference for the course of its development or for the reception it met with that it began its work on what is, of all the contents of the mind, most foreign to the ego – on symptoms. Symptoms are derived from the repressed, they are, as it were, its representatives before the ego; but the repressed is foreign territory to the ego – internal foreign territory – just as reality is external foreign territory.[5]

I did tell you, *this is what we had no knowledge of.* The power, kept hidden, of the Starting Point, in all our life experiences. Isn't it extraordinary? I exclaimed. My mother was impressed, my daughter carried away with enthusiasm. I brought her back to prudence: Revelation must be used wisely and with moderation. One must let it come. Now we can climb whenever we want. But we'll always have to *cultivate distance.* The grace of reaching the almost paradisiacal psychical space which Proust reaches via the 'clover- and artemisia-scented' road of Reading is granted us only on condition that we *Cultivate Distance.* Space out, inwardly and outwardly. Allow this mist of time which drapes this garden, this view over the sea, this walk at Versailles under the chestnut trees, of the shining reflection of the elusive which makes them look more beautiful to us than the rest of the world and as if immortalized, to form between people and things.

Let's return. That's the secret.

Let us travel the path of the Return without any consciousness of the time it is. It is the path of Reunions. And naturally it unfolds only if there are two of us teletreading it jointly.

It is time I returned to my subject, which is Philippine. Or Philippines. As I was trying to tell you about them, it, the word, I have spoken about something apparently totally different but the following Prologue is concerned with them. But before the Prologue, I owe you a confidence. When I started 'writing' this text, I thought it was called *Telepathic Garden* or *Lethepatic Garden*.

The names of texts,

where can they be coming from? This one, for example: *Philippine*. Or else *Dream I Tell You*? They arrive. By . . . tele-pathy-phony? What's certain is that they are not here, they are in inexistence during all the time when the text comes about and beyond time, until they wind up without a residence permit at my first reader's, who has always been Jacques Derrida. And who I suspect today continues to be so.

I acknowledge my *fateful*, almost neurotic incapacity to *give the name*. Maybe it is out of a fear of 'giving', as one says in idiomatic French, for giving over to the police, giving away, revealing the secret, betraying somebody. All the titles that come to my mind are fake titles. They ring false to my ear. *Faux, faut. Bon.*[6] Yet my texts do have titles, as they must [*il le faut*]? I am not responsible for them [*je n'en réponds pas*]. I've known for a long time, out of experience, that they are sent to me, they appear suddenly, whispered to me. Free from me. Imposing. I bow. This takes place according to a suggestion mechanism: Jacques Derrida reading the titleless thing from a distance, something in me is no doubt acted upon by the thread and wire [*fil*] of the telereading. A fishing line [*fil*] is cast out. As if I could hear Jacques Derrida mumble: 'yet another sea! Where on earth does she fish

18

that from?' Suddenly a word bites [*mot mord*]. His meta-phors. As if. One morning a name comes out. Sometimes several come forward in one and the same breath. One listens to them. I have no opinion. I side with him. Note that all this is foreign to me.

It is in the middle of the garden of the book, during the fine hours of an afternoon. I was unreading the Book which makes me cry. I had passed very often by those chapters. The word has been there. I was not looking for it. As always it responded to my desire even before that desire came to consciousness.

Philippine sprang up with the piercing authority of an arrow. I'm going to tell you everything. Is it a name? A word? One cannot imagine a more powerful (signifying) term. If I had looked for it, I would not have found it. It found me. The other day I was dashing, fast, flee-ing with impatience through the enclosed parks of a text with which I have a totally passionate relation, in a hurry to be done with suffering from it, to escape the repetition of a pain that has always been destined to be mine, being able neither to read it nor not to read it (other examples *Tristan and Isolde, Der Atem, Letters to Milena, The Legend of Saint Julian the Hospitaller*), one of those adored, yet feared books, without any literary charm to seduce me and protect me, and which do noth-ing but harm me with pinpoint accuracy. It is a cruel book, without the consolations lavished by sentences of a thrilling beauty. This took place all of a sudden – page 192. Here it is:

> The reality of our close companionship, of our true possession of each other (during our allotted time),

was absolute, complete, and thorough. No Darby that ever lived can ever have had sweeter, warmer, more tender memories of any Joan than I have now of Mary Seraskier! Although each was, in a way, but a seeming illusion of the other's brain, the illusion was no illusion for us. It was an illusion that showed the truth, as does the illusion of sight. Like twin kernels in one shell ('Philipschen,' as Mary called it), we touched at more points and were closer than the rest of mankind (with each of them a separate shell of his own). We tried and tested this in every way we could devise, and never found ourselves at fault, and never ceased to marvel at so great a wonder.[7]

Philippine. A word for two. A word worth two. A French word? A name word I had not heard for such a long time. It used to blossom in Algeria. Its fresh almond fragrance, freshness itself. Unbeknownst to me I immediately knew, received, that is to say, knew anew [*su, reçu, c'est-à-dire resu*]. To receive is to know anew what one used to know in another time. It means seeing a bygone time return.

I rang up my daughter straightaway. I wanted to share this with her. A Philippine has (always) two recipients by definition.

– Philippine, I said, do you know what it is?
– Philippine? No, I don't. Do *you* know?
I laughed
– Is it something obscene? she suggested.
I laughed. She laughed. Something obscene? Who knows?
Then I said:

– The almond. It's the almond. (I meant to say: it's the almond's lover [*l'amant de l'amande*] perhaps)

– It's an almond? How could I know this? Oh! it's an *amende*, a fine

– As well, I said

Aubergines[8] give philippines? That's what you mean? I am lost with my basket of fruit and vegetables

– If you write it with an *a*, you'll enjoy its taste.

– Oh! But I have never eaten philippines. What about you?

– Quite a few times.

– Where did you eat some then? In Algeria then?

– *At the starting point*, I said, there's always been some. In my opinion, you ate some.

– I would have eaten some philippines without knowing it?

– It's often the case. Philippine acts like Philtre. First one eats some. Then one forgets it. Then one is it.

Now I am going to tell you the secret of Philippine: it's an *amande* with an *a*. It's an almond with two almonds. One of the two almonds has to make amends [*frappée d'une amende*]. It follows by identification that the other also has to amend [*est frappée*]. It's a game of almonds. A double game. What is there in *Amande*? There is the double charm of an *âme* (soul) which summon*d*s [*mande*] two people not to forget each other, to call each other by the same name, to precede each other, to echo, dissociate and reflect each other

As if they were mutually almonding and amending each other [*se mettaient à l'amande mutuellement à l'amende*].

21

– Now I'm going to tell you what it is, I said: it's the title of my talk [*communication*].

– Of your talk?

– It's the title of thoughts talking to one another.

One says 'Philippine'. And all the thoughts ask: Philippine who? or what? And all the translators ask themselves how to translate Philippine in their language. Do you know what they call Philippine in English?

– It does not exist

– It cannot not exist. It crosses the Channel and when it gets to the other side, it's called Philippine. Nobody can doubt it. I made Telepathy with you. – You're in it in Philippine. – You've just put yourself in it. – You are my *Fillipine* (Philippine daughter).

Now I make Philippine with myself

What does Philippine tell me? I have Philippine on the cordial Telephone. Telephilia. Telephilippine.

Oh so many things. And then so many things. One opens.

But *who* is Philippine?

This is a question I did not ask myself. It calls me

– Who calls me?

– Hello, it's me! – Oh! I recognize you. Your voice among all the voices.

Philippine is me is you! You know the rite. The fate. An enchanted almond. It contains the *worlds*[9] in its shell. Plato's world: it alone sums up the *Symposium*, its myth of Love, its tragedy. One has forgotten it a little? Now the myth of the androgyne revealed itself to Plato one day in the Symposium [*Banquet*] when he was sharing bread and

22

fruit with a dear friend. Which of the two *philoi* found it? They were eating almonds. Those fruits with the velvety hull which do not give themselves to the first thief that comes along. Those mothers who conceal the soft, sweet child. The outer almond resists the hasty predator, says Plato. This is how desire is kept alive, through the toughness of the approach. The inner almond has the shape of a delicate oval which is used as a model and a reference to what is beautiful: a sea shell, a pearl, the lover's [*amante*] eyes, everything that resembles a sublime tear is almond-shaped. Even Christ in glory, even the Virgin, are entrusted to the soft oval frame of an almond. The Virgin herself in the mandorla shines softly as a *mystical almond.*

From almond to almond the almond enshrines itself, promises itself, steals away, receives, an emblematic fruit of hospitality, host and hostess, passive and active, chaste and destined to be peeled, as I am doing now by opening the envelope of its names. Philippine is the androgynous almond. It always thinks about love.

Right here, in this very moment, Philia my cat comes and lays her paws on this page. As has been known since Ovid, cats are telepathic. Aletheia follows immediately. They guessed I was going to think about them. While I am making amends, the thought that the magic almonds from the market in rue des Juifs came to our home, 54 rue Philippe in Oran, on Fridays, returns to my mind.

I never think of *thinking* of rue Philippe for I walk along it in a dream where I use it as my inner street whenever I go to the far end of the town up to the building behind which, if one were to walk round it, one would glimpse the sea eternally.

Now everything urges me to make Philippine with my

brother. We are sitting side by side. – In order to enrich your book, says my brother, I'm going to tell you my dream. In my dream I am younger. Our seventy years are behind me. I am seven years old. It's very pleasant.

– Philippine, I say.

– For us Philippines are the double or twin almonds [*amandes jumelles*], he says. When we were kids, we felt we were very lucky. He says. (Instead of the almond, three mouthfuls of bread with three thick layers of jam like that.) One no longer eats young almonds here. It's an abandoned fruit. – You've never made Philippine in France? – Never. – It's a matter of age as well. The Philippine joy. It's a childish Surprise.

First one thinks it's Greek. It's Greek. One opens. There is more than one almond in the almond. The Al(e)manic [*l'alemande*] is held within the almond. Shall one open? Let's open the dictionary.[10] The first A(l)emanic who says Philippine is German [*allemande*]. It's the marvellous Surprise. In fact Philippine is the altered form, through *attraction* of the first name *Philippe*, of the German word *Vielliebchen*. My much loved little one my dear little beloved my darling androgyne, me-you miaow [*mimoi mitoi minou*], my fellow tenant in love. What lovely sworn words [*juremots*] these false twins [*jumeaux*] are, aren't they? Who will tell us the secrets of the force of attraction?

Mandorla. Why have I never forgotten this song by Celan?

MANDORLA
In der Mandel – was steht in der Mandel?
Das Nichts.

Es steht das Nichts in der Mandel.
Da steht es und steht.

Im Nichts – wer steht da? Der König.
Da steht der König, der König.
Da steht er und steht.

Judenlocke, wirst nicht grau.

Und dein Aug – wohin steht dein Auge?
Dein Aug steht der Mandel entgegen.
Dein Aug, dem Nichts stehts entgegen.
Es steht zum König.
So steht es und steht.

Menschenlocke, wirst nicht grau.
Leere Mandel, königsblau.

MANDORLA

In the almond – what dwells in the almond?
Nothing.
What dwells in the almond is Nothing.
There it dwells and dwells.

In Nothing – what dwells there? The King.
There the King dwells, the King.
There he dwells and dwells.

Jew's curl, you'll not turn grey.

And your eye – on what does your eye dwell?
On the almond your eye dwells.

Your eye, on Nothing it dwells.
Dwells on the King, to him remains loyal, true.
So it dwells and dwells.

Human curl, you'll not turn grey.
Empty almond, royal-blue.[11]

Thus Philippe will have attracted and seduced Vielliebchen while Philippine is attracted by Vielliebchen, but actually nobody will ever be able to say who first attracted whom, *it's the mystery of transference.*

In the end this chapter is called *Télépatitre.*

– I was about to call you! you say. I was calling you. I am calling you, my hand on the telephone, Telepathy the Accomplice Goddess, the switchboard operator expert in simultaneous talks makes thought think of thought at the very second. There is no second. The speed is the speed of light. It is you, in the garden, even when you are not there, this emission of overluminous light, this radio breath in the foliage of hornbeams. Hardly have we passed each other the word than already the word is past, spontaneously. *File.* You say to me *File.*

Sometimes you say nothing, you only just beam radiantly. I can hear everything you think. I answer. I try to justify myself. My radiance is less strong than yours. It's to listen to you all the better.

The distance between us is supple, reflexible and obeys our moods. When we are cross it pretends to thicken. A smile and it turns into a puddle of sun.

Every one of us has a secret book. It is a book with a secret lock [*à secret*]. Holding secrets [*à secrets*]. We don't talk about it.

It is a cherished book. It is not beautiful. Not great. Not so well written, sometimes not very well written even. We don't care. For it is goodness itself for us. The absolute friend. The first and the last. It promises and lives up to what it promises. It is modest, solid, profound. We forget it but it never forgets us. It knows everything about us but it does not know it knows. We do not know what it knows but we know it knows. If Freud had been asked to name his secret(ive) book, he would not have hesitated: it would have been *The Jungle Book*.[12] In its forest, I dare say, lives the one he will always have called 'our hero'.

You notice this turn of phrase? He says that with a sort of amused distance, in Voltaire's or in Sterne's style, intruding metadiegetically into the narrative, as if he wanted to debunk the ideality of their puppet, to mock them a little with the reader as accomplice: *our hero who does not see he is not a hero*, you see? – But no, it's not that. This lightness is all pretence. You can hear the slight inflection in his voice, this note of tenderness which it is advisable to dissimulate. Our hero, however ridiculous he may sometimes be, is you but he is mostly me. Here is our Freud, like Norbert Hanold, the mentally myopic, who suddenly recognizes himself in the canary locked up in a cage. 'Our hero', what a sign! Someone we know well creeps under the plumage of this clichéd form. Why do we follow so passionately this crank of an armchair archeologist, this asinanalyst [*ânalyste*] with a dunce's cap [*bonnet d'âne*] who mistakes women for statues and takes to the street in his nightgown at noon, if not because we are him. It's me-me, mini-me, a small cock reared up on its ego spurs [*ergots*], it's the petty king who wants to become big, it's ego. It's Gogo.

Gogo, what a name for the one who will be our hero! An impossible name. Besides nobody remembers it.

The one book Proust loved above all others was *Le Capitaine Fracasse*. I have never read it. Proust might have read the book which makes me weep. I myself never read it: I dream it. I live it again. This book about which you've seen me thinking for a while, as if I could see its two characters, sitting in the corner of the hall, gently holding hands, this book with almost supernatural powers, which no wall, no distance prevents from mingling its breaths with my words, this book which is as marvellous for me as *Le Capitaine Fracasse* remained marvellous for Proust even after he forgot it, no doubt its title will seem as foreign to you as the character of the Capitaine Fracasse is to me, and I will just utter this loud-sounding name here: *Peter Ibbetson*. I hold it as dear as the apple of my eye, just as I hold dear the condition, the law, the grace, of my whole life: the gift of dreaming true.

I could have thought about it: isn't this book some sort of fortune-telling book[13] for me?

I never think about it. It knows too much. I have always refrained from exploring it. It is enough that I feel it sparkling behind me, pearl after pearl, while I go to my dreams. It occurs to me today that

this Peter has a twin sister. She is Gradiva. Today is the first time I become aware of the links between them.

28

The two books were born at a distance and at the same time, each in a different language. Perhaps from an undiagnosed telepathy

In a way they tell the same story. It is about death and resurrection. The author? now he is called George du Maurier, now he is called Wilhelm Jensen, the author has a similar stroke of genius. This stroke of genius is so strong that it can take place only once. Genius is stronger than the author. Same for the Apocalypse. The illumination takes place only once. So that it can be said that there is no author any longer. The Book of Revelation is dictated by a telepathic act. 'The author' will have been the medium for a manifestation of supernatural forces. The two 'authors' in question are true conductors of these thunderstriking phenomena. This is why they will have been struck only once. The whole irradiating truth is gathered in the destiny of one single creature, Peter or Gradiva. This is what is called a thunderstroke: the real stroke is always unique. This is why the end is in the beginning: there can be no other hero of the revelation than Romeo – with Juliet. Here they are, from one second to the next, hurled forever into the same psychical space. What takes place? During the initial collision, there is a transference of the seat of life to the place of the other. This can be compared to a *postnatal twinship*. Each makes the life of the other. It's a great strength. It's a great vulnerability. The first who dies kills the other by transmission.

The author? Almost nobody. He will only have managed to be the ghost servant of the great Peter Ibbetson. It is said that this George du Maurier, who knew how to draw but not how to write, proposed (suggested) to his friend Henry James that he should make his literary portrait. That of Peter Ibbetson. But nobody can write my autobiography in my place.

George du Maurier expected from Henry James the impossible gift of a self-analysis. According to Freud he was not wrong. Literary geniuses are those soothsayers who act involuntarily, spontaneously, from a distance over minds paralysed by laziness by restoring, without knowing how – by *incitations*, says Proust, by intimations, by prophetic promise – desire, intoxication, the power to want to go beyond the canvas on which the last or first reflection of a vision vibrates indistinctly. Now George du Maurier's call to Henry James produced the effect he had hoped for. It all happened as if Henry James had asked George du Maurier (to write) to paint the inner picture around which George du Maurier had been roaming forever and whose charm remained undecipherable to him. It is the ghost of Henry James in him which called him to lift partially the piece of green canvas which offered to him the reflection of a fixed mirage. Only Henry James and only Henry James's refusal could help him to venture beyond its surface, only this foreign intervention could compel him to reinsert himself into the life of his mind, where he suddenly found again the way which leads to an endlessly magnificent vision. *Peter Ibbetson* is the book by Henry James which he did not write.

Peter Ibbetson calls me. It's me here, Psyche, memory and unmirror [*démiroir*] of Psyche the first. In reality though, I was not yet, at least that's what I believe. It is as if I were reading my memoirs. Thus I would have already lived this, one century before I was actually born.[14]

I alone can have a foreboding of the way I will die.

I can ask nobody to think in my place what will likely happen to me one day through the very fact of being predicted. And yet when I meet Peter Ibbetson, it's always the first time in appearance, and I sense that 'there', it is as if all about me, all that I do not know, were known. There shudders a foreign memory in which my lost memory wanders as in a dream.

I have already been in this garden but I don't know I have.

When one day I know, when I recognize my garden, I will ask myself, but in vain, how Peter Ibbetson's garden will have been able, at a distance in time and space, to be the dazzling prefiguration of the Garden of the Cercle Militaire.

Peter Ibbetson says something to me

Is it a book? What is a book? This cherished book, do I read it? What am I doing when I lock myself with it in a feverish tête-à-tête from which I cannot wrench myself? I get up ten times, I get ready to pay a visit to my friends, I am dressed, I return to the book, I am summoned, bewitched, held back by the mysterious forces of Reading. I can hear its siren's murmur: *Let's return to the starting point*, come on, come with me. And that's what I want above all: I want a book to make itself dream [*fasse rêve*] and bring me back to childhoods: infancy, the first, second, fourth, etc. childhood. To read is nothing but that, is it not? To return to oneself in prehistory in those legendary times when we were toddling and

31

telepathing round the world on all fours and eight paws [*à quatre pattes et huit télépathes*] to see where its opening was. As always for those expeditions, the traveller must be able to have at his disposal in the book these magic primitive objects which will enable him to establish radio links with legendary times. Starting for me with: a Gate. And also: a Garden. One keeping (watch over) the other. There is a child.

What does Peter Ibbetson say to me?
Go! Go![15] Move on! Move on
Peter Ibbetson, you say. Which one? For there are two *Peter Ibbetson*s which make philippine from a distance, one being the one who dreams, the other the one who is dreamt, one returning from the other, to the other. If I muse about it [*songe*], it so happens that *Peter Ibbetson* the first, the one who brought me to tears, with which I first found myself behind bars, will have been the next *Peter Ibbetson*,

It was the most beautiful film in the world. I persuaded myself easily that the Severed One, the recluse, was a copy of my father. But I'm not going to talk here about the transference love I always felt for Gary *Cooper*.[16] For sure re*cuper*ated by the father [*à tous les coups le père*]?

This film was not a film, I want to make it clear. It's a vision. It's a Revelation which will have exceeded all the calculations of its creators. For the true authors of this Vision, of this Dream filmed in a state of dream, are quite obviously the adorable Inventors of the Dreaming True, the Great Dreamed Ones whose names are sometimes Peter and Mary, but not always. As they have the gift of truedreaming [*rêvance vraie*], it follows that, like all those invited in dreams, they have transfigureal names and figures. They are themselves mistaken, fail to know themselves, tremble with emotion, which allows them to taste the painful happiness of double love. Of dual love. Under the borrowed names, under the new bodies which lead them astray, under the foliage whose French look conceals the fabulous forest of *A Midsummer Night's Dream*, they are subjected to the laws of a strange attraction. The everlasting childhood which plays within them on the ruins of names thwarts the prisons and towers of lost time. But before the narrative there has been a first narrative. I have forgotten it completely, behind the dream. In this first narrative the two children who have invented names, Gogo and Mimsey, are always watched over by their invisible doubles, Prince Charming and the fairy Tarapatapoum, two fairy-like genii who will follow them incognito all their lives. Only they have the secret. These two, Charm and Tarapathypoum, live in the French language. They are accompanied by a true dream dog in French, the childhood dog, which of course is called Médor. Each time one of them shouts *Médor*, that is to say *Mais dors* (do sleep), the other one echoes: *mais je dors* (but I am sleeping). I am already waiting for you. Come quick.

Nobody still remembers that as a child George du Maurier had as truly fateful a neighbour as the little girl whose eyes were so black that for the eyes of the future narrator of the *Recherche* they could be nothing but blue. A Gilberte, for it could only be her, on the other side of the gates, called him Gogo. That's my guess at least.

Gogo is the ring of the golden bell which announces Mamma's coming for the evening kiss. The kiss of the first love.

There is the Child, I mean Childhood, I mean the Genie or Genius, the little defenceless child who is still in the state of superhuman Clairvoyance

Ever since I have begun returning to my starting point, the ghosts return to greet me, as always in the case of ghosts, they were eagerly waiting: they are always here, they hold out their tender arms to me, I pass them by without seeing them. They vanish out of melancholy. At the slight sign of waking, they arrive, happy . . .

The other day I had my apocalypse. I was dreamily skimming through the depths of Proust's unpublished Prefaces. Everything seemed to me so far and so near, I could have said, like Proust echoing Flaubert: 'That was in Megara, a suburb of Carthage, in Hamilcar's gardens', when I saw at the top of a page a child hopping on three upturned stones. I startled with joy. With a happiness found again. Yet I was awake. But the child! A boy who is dead and yet answers to each pressing gaze, who just asks to be resurrected! Oh! I recognized him, as one recognizes one day in a Museum, looming out of a painting, the loved dog once lost, the-child-who-plays-within-me-on-the-ruins, and it was *the first time* I came and surrendered to him. It is as if, at last, *I saw him by heart.*

> [. . .] it is often when I am most sick, when I have no ideas left in my head nor any strengths left, that this ego which I sometimes recognize catches sight of the links between two ideas, just as it is often in autumn, when there are no more flowers or leaves, that one senses the most profound harmonies in landscapes. And this boy who thus plays in me on the ruins needs no food, he

merely feeds on the pleasure afforded him by the vision of the idea he discovers, he creates it, it creates him, he dies, but an idea resurrects him, like those seeds which stop germinating in too dry an atmosphere and which are dead: but a little humidity and warmth is enough to resurrect them.[17]

I had already seen that child so often on the page of a book. It always seemed to me it was another. Each time. Whenever I saw a child, it was for the first time. He interested me passionately. He reminded me of nobody. I recognized him. Yet I can see myself following him immediately in a street where the most sparkling life meets death. I did not think of the child Thomas Bernhard who steps on a child's-hand-ripped-off-a-child in bombed Salzburg's Gstätengasse. I did not think of Heathcliff. Yet I had not forgotten him.

All those children who inhabit books, who play within me in books, in ruins

He is always there, eternally, playing in the ruins, me

Why did I not recognize him? 'I did not make the connection,' as one says without knowing what one says. I am, I believe, a grown-up who looks at the ephemeral inhabitant from another time. What a mistake! The eternal being is the child. The grown-up is the ghost. It is the child who dreams, thinks, senses the world, and who is the genius. Poor Grown-Up. The *true* is the one who seemed to me to be other, another.

It took me some time to receive the message, myself. Yet did Jacques Derrida not say that the one who personally receives the letter in secret [*au secret*] is the one to whom it is destined. *Sero te amaui* always, one has known since Augustine that what is (too) late is the law of truth. Besides I had received it and I had not recognized it. At each encounter I had trembled, cried my heart out, felt the convulsions of compassion, the pains of disconsolateness.

Who, in *Peter Ibbetson*, is the most foreign stranger?

One does not recognize oneself.

One is oneself the lost child, the orphan, the one without roots, the hostage of a forgetting, of an arrested memory.

A boy?

If it wasn't you, then it was your brother.[18] Who is the joyful shining ghost who does not yet see death coming?

My father? My brother? My son? therefore Me

It is like the lost, abandoned child in *Peter Ibbetson*. Peter Ibbetson? What an unusual name. I bet son?[19] Or else Ibn?[20]

Peter Ibbetson left behind him, on the other side of the Channel – of which Jacques Derrida told us that it can keep silent[21] – in a fabulous garden, a little boy who is no longer called Gogo. Gogo is done for. Gogo is gone.[22] One fine day all was lost: father, mother, country, language, name, Mimsey, garden, cart, Médor, passwords . . . All crossed out. Cancelled. Only the ruins remain in the garden kept imprinted in its full glory.

My Uncle Ibbetson [. . .] took to me [. . .] I had to change my name [. . .]

So Pierre Pasquier de la Marière, *alias* Monsieur Gogo, became Master Peter Ibbetson, and went to Bluefriars, the gray-coat school, where he spent six years – [. . .]

I hated the garb, I hated the surroundings – the big hospital at the back, and that reek of cruelty, drunkenness, and filth, the cattle-market – where every other building was either a slaughter-house, a gin-palace, or a pawnbroker's shop, more than all I hated the gloomy jail opposite, where they sometimes hanged a man in public on a Monday morning. This dismal prison haunted my dreams when I wanted to dream of Passy, of my dear dead father and mother and Madame Seraskier.

For the first term or two they were ever in my thoughts, and I was always trying to draw their profiles on desks and slates and copybooks, till at last all resemblance seemed to fade out of them; and then I drew M. le Major till his side face became quite demoralized and impossible, and ceased to be like anything in life. Then I fell back on others: le Père François, with his eternal *bonnet de colon* and sabots stuffed with straw; the dog Médor, the rocking-horse, and all the rest of the menagerie; the diligence that brought me away from Paris; the heavily jack-booted couriers in shiny hats and pigtails, and white breeches, and short-tailed blue coats covered with silver buttons, who used to ride through Passy, on their way to and fro between the Tuileries and St. Cloud, on little, neighing, gray stallions with bells round their necks and tucked-up tails, and beautiful heads like the horses' heads in the Elgin Marbles.

In my sketches they always looked and walked and trotted the same way: to the left, or westward as it would be on the map. M. le Major, Madame Seraskier, Médor, the diligences and couriers, were all bound westward by common consent – all going to London, I suppose, to look after me, who was so dotingly fond of them.[23]

The work of erasure – engraving through the striking sketch will have begun as a response to a triple imprisonment. One recognizes the story of the sketch's origin, Dibutade's invention. I too, when my father dies, during the few days of his dying in secret [*mourance au secret*], I quickly write a book in order to block up the broken pane with a piece of paper. Each time the child in me wants to communicate with my father, she turns towards the paper screen hung in front of the torn pane behind which my father walks far away – no, he is far away, caught again, pulled towards disappearance he goes away, like a condemned man, his face turned towards me. It is very mild in the deserted garden. A bed of violets gives out its fragrance, for nobody anymore, and she waits. She does not know for whom or for what. Until it comes, *the Voice*. She listens, she responds. That's what her telepathy is about: there is always a device which serves as a cause and a prop, to programme the sending and receiving, the recimission of the missive, a canvas-screen to project the ghosts' silhouettes, flies, a ruin in the grown-up . . .

N.B.: It works only *from a distance*. Only if it is *crypted*. Veiled in mistery [*brume-étrange*]. If I were conscious, this would not occur. But it always takes place unbeknownst to me. Linen, percale, matting, canvas between Peter and me.

Having recognized him once does not interrupt the magic of the haunting fear [*hantise*]. It's the same for dreams: no light will ever manage to breach the fertile darkness.

The summer radiance stops me short. We lived on rue Philippe. At this very moment my brother, the other inhabitant of rue Philippe, is making a phone call. – You were thinking of rue Philippe, Pete? I say. – Not at all.

Pete, I never called him Pierre. Pete is his telepythic name.

Granted, my brother *was not thinking* of rue Philippe when he was at the other end of the line that morning. But *he was there*. As the perfectly peaceful and natural tone of his voice can testify. He himself was not at all surprised that I was there, and he caught up with me that very instant by telephone, in the midst of the racket on rue de Paris along which he was walking while talking to us. – Pete, I said . . . – Hélène you're round about? Near rue Philippe? – At the corner of rue du Cercle Militaire. We will soon be seen coming down hand in hand, walking alongside the tall, elaborately carved iron gates, with pounding hearts, pulled by the same ardent mental reservation as we are hastening towards the tall portal which gives scant access to this Eden in Oran. With all our exalted souls we present our lives in front of the Entrance. – Curiously, says my brother, I have never called you anything other than Hélène. I have never found a diminutive. Pete ponders. I remember trying. More than once. I remember attempting. But I could not find anything. I tried Échelle (ladder) but it did not work. Hélène, Échelle. Lame [*un échec*]. You can't get everything right in life.

We first attempted to enter the Garden of the Cercle Militaire in Oran. Afterwards, in Algiers, we attempted [*essayâmes*] the Jardin d'Essai.

My brother has forgotten the Gates.

The Gates summon me to answer. Aim at me. Hit me.

My culture gates, my fantasy gates. The gates in *Peter Ibbetson*.

In the first scene of *Peter Ibbetson* the two children are in full glory. The mandorla where they meet in the double enclosure of two beautiful equal gardens is framed by a predella featuring a detailed representation of Eden.[24] One would almost think it is a divine dream. The separations exist only to make reunions more delicious and fragrant. I have known this double garden. The two children pass from one compartment of the predella to the other with the grace of birds. Like two squirrels. In this world before time we are naturally bilingual, we speak masculine-feminine, French to English and both languages like angels. We call each other funny little secret idiotic names: the two children are called Mimsey and Gogo, these are their philippines' names in the Garden. The little girl always asked to be carried by Gogo (for they called me thus, *without any reason actually*, since my first name was Pierre, says Peter Ibbetson in brackets).

These are *nothing but* loan proper names in which the last word is concealed, the word of fate, the flip word [*mot qui file*]. Nowhere else but there, in the ensnaring lakes [*lacs*] of letters, does the key to fate conceal itself, Jacques Derrida would say, when he roamed on the edge of the invisible lake called Telepathy, at the risk of a faux-pas, more than a forbidden *faut pas*[25] of course. Why, does he ask himself, in my reveries of suicide is it always drowning which imposes itself, and most often in a *lake*, sometimes a pond but usually a lake? Nothing is stranger to me than a lake: too far from the landscapes of my childhood. Maybe it's literary instead? I think it's more the force of the word, *lac*. Something in it overturns or precipitates (*cla, alc*), plunging down head first. You will say that in these words, in their letters, I want to disappear, not necessarily in order to die there but to live there concealed, perhaps In order to dissimulate what I know. So *glas*, you see, would have to be tracked down thereabouts (*cla, cl, clos, lacs, le lacs, le piège, le lacet, le lais, là, da, fort, hum* . . . [cla, cl, closed, lakes, snare, trap, gin, the silt, there, yes, strong, hum . . .]). Had I spoken to you about 'Claude'? You will remind me, I must tell you who this name is for me. You will note that it is androgynous, like *poste*, I missed it in *Glas*, but it has never been far away, *it* has not missed me. The catastrophe is of this name.[26]

There is nothing but lake [lac]. Something in the lake attracts him, promises him to keep him hidden, in the cellarage [*cale*], concealed. One recognizes that fellow in the cellarage.[27] Each drowns under the floor of time according to their primitive water, each returns to their originary sea or pool. 'Our hero', in the days of Gogo before being transferred into Peter Ibbetson, dreamt of drowning in the pool at Auteuil among the people of salamanders and dytiscus, of saurians and batrachians, all these fabulous prehistoric animals endowed, as is well known, with that ability most desired by human beings: *regeneration*.

One must *dive* to the bottom of the pond in order to re-member oneself

When I myself dive each night, I do so driven by the urgency to find again the extraordinary regenerative power of dreams, the a(na)chronic state in which what has been destroyed is brought back into life.

But not everybody is a *dutikos*.[28]

Telepathics is also a dutics.

Forgotten. I have completely forgotten that Proust was born in Auteuil on 10 July 1871 at 96 rue de La Fontaine. What if he had met Peter Ibbetson in the neighbouring gardens or on the edge of the old 'Fontis', where he said he only caught hay fever? I can still hear him murmuring 'This Auteuil of my childhood – of my childhood and of his youth' which he evokes and I can understand that he delights in taking his mind back to it as to all that has migrated from the visible world into the invisible.

This Auteuil of my childhood – of my childhood and of his youth – evoked by Jacques Blanche, I can understand that he delights in taking his mind back to it as to all that has migrated from the visible world into the invisible, to all that, converted into memories, gives some sort of additional value to our thought, shadowed by arbours that no longer exist. But that Auteuil interests me still more as a same tiny corner of the earth which can be observed across two fairly distant ages of its Time travel.[29]

It has returned? Without explanation. Auteuil is as foreign to me as the lake for Jacques Derrida. I do not know which messenger has brought to my attention this notice about the births of ghosts of dear children which took place in this imaginary country where later I will find myself in Oran on rue du Cercle Militaire crushed by heat like Gradiva at noon in Pompeii.

Is this telepathy? Pompeiipathy perhaps. *Pompe* had been waiting for me, a word I had stopped liking – a long time ago, ever since it became funeral [*funèbre*],[30] at my father's garden. I always pass by rue de la Pompe without thinking. When Peter Ibbetson evokes rue de la Pompe I pass (it over). And yet *Pompe* does not lack resources, *Pompé* (pumped) is at once the sending and what is sent. *Pompe* as pomp and *Pompe* as pump are philippines. One makes a procession, escorts. The other carries the sub-terranean water. The one accompanies the visible. The other the invisible.

In the film the family on the mother's side of divine Mme Seraskier is not called Biddulph. It is called Forsyte. When I think I notice this one day, I dare not believe it. As I never 'see' this film unless in a state of hypnosis, perhaps I have invented it, grafted it? Forsyte? Why? It's too good to be true. I consider checking. I refrain. Uncertainty has its charm. What if I had been mistaken? Why should it be Mme Seraskier who was born Forsyte and not Biddulph? I am pressed by a flock of questions. I will have imagined all that? Then I would have been under the suggestion of Freuderrida. The case of the Forsyte case which has been pursuing Freud in via di Mercurio in Vienna since one morning in the autumn of 1919 at 11.45 am – which he notes, sows, decides to take with him to the Harz in 1921 in order to present it to his close friends, which he then discovers he has 'forgotten', takes place in Gastein, which transforms the Forsyte case into the case of the forgettable unforgettable. Thus he will have 'obeyed' a powerful, involuntary movement of 'Resistance', that is to say, of alterobedience by autodisobedience, turning a parapraxis [*acte manqué*] into telepathic fireworks. All the indicators are on in the Freudian brain. With its double charge of twisted autosuggestion, the case of the Forsyte case exercises an undeniable seduction over any reader spectator. Thus this paradoxical blind Fore-sight (1) eludes any attempt at being put in the service of a public analytic proposition since each evocation provokes its omission. It still cannot be found at the required moment in 1921, and is replaced at the last minute by anything whatsoever. (2) In another time the case returns with the *Unheimlich* power which infiltrates the narrative annexes and ploys used to escort and heighten works of fiction with such a high rate of unconscious incidents (one could cite *Wuthering Heights* or *Peter Ibbetson*) that they seem to call for the faked help of a witness guaranteed to be 'normal' and impervious to inner foreign messages. The account of the case of the case is then located on the threshold of the fake lecture known as 'Psycho-Analysis and Telepathy'. Therefore inside-outside. At the portal. But I lose my way as is predicted and programmed by the genius of distance, of tele- or of *Vor-* or of For, *Fort* or *Fors*. Thus it is in 1922 or 1932 or else in 1941 that the Ghost case settles in front of the portal of the Dreamer's house, which is the spitting image of the Portal of the house at Auteuil.[31]

Struck by the inexplicable resemblances between all these fortuitous elements foreign to one another, I will have thus reintroduced the Forsyte leitmotif into the film, like a graft of signifier in a dream? But also as the symptom of my own secret battle against the Amnesias which harass my life in the other world, and chase me like spectral Furies whose fatal apparitions I fear. Now, among the feared cryptonyms, I have long learnt to recognize the revenant *Forgetting of the name Forsythia*. But one day, while watching *from a distance* and absent-mindedly the 'film' which my daughter follows attentively, I hear the unquestionable jingle of the golden syllables falling one by one and vanishing. This is at the fifteenth minute of the hallucination. The precision to the minute is comparable to the precision of the schedule of the handing over to Freud of the card of Dr David Forsyth who has just arrived from London at this very moment.[32]

The clock cannot be suspected of memory disorder.

Where shall we meet again/find ourselves back [*nous retrouverons-nous*]?

At the corner of *rue de la Tour* and of *rue de la Pompe*. We are getting near the tall iron gates. At the corner of rue Philippe and of rue du Cercle Militaire. One more step – and it will not be a dream any longer but something else, a kind of –

New Life –

Life within Life – dream beyond the dream

Will have begun.

I am going towards the First Step

Peter Ibbetson will have spent [*passé*] almost all his foreign outer life in prison. In reality. As a being with two languages and with two lives, he always takes place [*se passe*] in reality and in true reality at the same time, in prison and in true paradise, in reality, in the same reality. It's not a dream. The true dream is dreamt true to him in full reality at the same time as it is dreamt true by the Duchess of Towers

I only need to take one glance at this immense book to glimpse its gateways [*grilles*] of reading: everything – space, time, narrow paths and magnificent prospects – is commanded in two languages joined by towers and gates.[33] This shibboleths via incredible linguistic magics. Thus the note of the inner music, the spiritual music of this telepathic gospel, is the omnipotent soft word 'true'. Now the musical soul of 'true' is *tour*.[34]

The Duchess of Towers shares Peter Ibbetson's lot as together they jump over all the fateful bars: bars of mournings, bars of contretemps, of jails, of laws, of gallows, of deaths. Radiant mistress of mysteries. It is not easy to dream true. One must learn the technique and obey the rules to the letter. But it is not impossible.

One of the conditions for the true dream:

Out there, through that park, [. . .] – there's a gap in the hedge you can get through; but mind and make everything plain in front of you – *true*, before you go a step farther, or else you'll have to wake and begin it all over again. You have only to will it, and think of yourself as awake, and it will come – on condition, of course, that you have been there before.

[. . .] you must never for a moment cease thinking of where you want to be in your dream till you are asleep and get there; and you must never forget in your dream where and what you were when awake. You must join the dream on to reality.[35]

In reality they dream. Reality is the dream. The dream is the true reality.

As you're listening to me, you think you're dreaming. One must imagine this: they dream their lives, they are not dreamt, they twin-dream their dreams, they copilot, they codream, the codreamers.

They dream about/by life, they live by dream [*ils rêvent à la vie, ils vivent au rêve*]

They snatch time away, they lay bare the bars

They remove belief and incredulity

They are overthrowers

What we call 'the day' on our side – busy day, day of entertainment – glides over their feathers like a meaningless dream – and the whole force of the true life blossoms in the powerful other-reality of the dream dreamt by two (dreamers)

Why have I always responded to *Peter Ibbetson* and to Peter Ibbetson as if *this lesson in dreaming true* were addressed to me?

My apocalypse takes place the moment I write this. I hear inwardly (but what does 'inwardly' mean?) Jacques Derrida responding to me in the same second, the very second, it seems to me, 'there is only autoteleanalysis'.[36]

'What are you saying?' I exclaimed. I recognize the little anguished exaltation which lights up each time I hear his voice telephoning to my thought the lost key words he can see me looking for everywhere. If you receive like a present the chance of these names, it is because you find yourself unknowingly on his line of transference.

Dream or not, I am receiving.

It is only when I write that light filters through the shutters. As if the Duchess of Towers taught me how *to read* the secret hidden in the name inscribed in letters of gold on the portico. Read.

'Peter Ibbetson' remained for years a familiar, foreign, inert, obsessive, immutable opaque body, whose dry sounds jarred my ear, which was associated with nothing, did not play, felt heavy, had no lock, the air could not get through, it did not rhyme, it resisted me or else I resisted it. Just lead. Until that day in spring when I wrote it out. Then suddenly, under the light gliding of my pen, the name livens up, breathes, sparkles. The casket delivers its contents:

At last, through the mesh, I saw: PeteR IbbetSON
Pr i son.
I found it, nobody can doubt it.

Thus Prison is in Peter Ibbetson, whereas Peter Ibbetson is in prison, destinally!

I nearly wept with emotion. What prevented me from doing so was my mother. She has the knack of barging in at the most decisive moments, as if umbilical communication were never interrupted. In the past I used to flinch. Not to be able to cut off the line, to see my mother suddenly appear in my tragedies and rummage in my drawers offended me. Now I appreciate her connections of an additional line. So, hardly had I exclaimed: my prison! when my mother entered. – I've received a box of explosives! I am not sure if it is allowed, said Ève. And she lays on my imprisonment warrant a box of chocolates [*bouchées*]. Chocolate explosives. Whereas I was in my imaginary jail.

And what if Ève were my Duchess of Towers? in reality? The one who gives me a strong hand, twice stronger than mine

What is strange is the reversal of one philippine into another. In the garden of the Duchess of Towers, I am in Pierre's place, Gogo the captive who dreams is me. Peter's despair is mine. And the voice of Mary, alias Mimsey, alias life itself, it depends, it is the voice of the being with whom I am in inner respondance [*répondance*], who holds me back just before I sink, and in front of whom bars vanish. Whereas I am always *behind* bars, on the other side.

Let's return to the straw upon which Peter Ibbetson lies and dreams in reality. Light comes in, carved by the thick bars of the cell. Thus I have always been at home, in my inner foreign country, the one my uncle Freud talks about – without recognizing it, I was inside, so much so that I did not know I was, I was blind in *Peter Ibbetson* I was in my fateful blinding exactly in a sunstruck state which projected me outside myself into the other world, when I passed as a child from the philippine darkness to the dazzling explosion of the Cercle Philippine. I have never been so blind – so visionary [*voyante*], so blindly clairvoyant as in Oran. I could see reality in all its truths hidden in it like secret entries in cryptonyms, I was always on the other side, I was always with prison, I was walking round, I never knew whether I was walking round the inside of the wall or whether I was walking round the wall on the outside, I was apprisoned [*aprisonnée*], bound to the existence of a state of prison and therefore of freedom of mind.

Now prison is all the more powerful since it presents itself under the figure of a desirable place, of an attractive foreign body, with enchanting features, everybody knows that.

One wants to enter it. On the other hand one is afraid of it.

'In such cases as these, only the first step is costly.' Somebody makes me think that.

I return to my first steps. I learnt how to dream before learning how to write. This can be learnt. One must have a few accessories at one's disposal. Some suggest an outer or inner desert. A stone [*pierre*]. A stuffed parrot [*perroquet*] (that is to say, a *pierroquet*). Stones that speak by suggestion. A perch for the Holy Spirit. That is to say, for me a ladder

First traps [*feintes*], first gaps [*fentes*]

when I was three years old in Oran, rue Philippe and at the corner of rue du Cercle Militaire. At irregular intervals I received a message from the night. From time to time the night would send on to the ceiling of my bedroom with closed shutters the fluid spectre of a ladder made up of bars of luminosity and bright shadow. The ladder ran slowly on the ceiling, descended on the white

50

wall opposite my bed and vanished. A car had driven past on the cobbled roadway. I was keeping the ladder. I called it back on the wall, raised it up to the ceiling, took it quickly, and called a dream

At the corner of the street there was a ladder with vertical bars which unfurled its spears all along the enclosure of the True Garden. But I still had not made the junction between these bars, some horizontal, others vertical.

'If one gets accustomed to the idea of telepathy, he wrote, all of a sudden, our hero of the fictional *New Lectures*, alias Freud, one can use it on a grand scale [*échelle*], but actually in imagination only.'

This telepathic ladder or scale with immense, still mysterious but undeniable powers, you will find it erected in the middle of the famous true-false, truly apocalyptical new lecture called 'Dream and Occultism' (where the extraordinary event takes place, which Jacques Derrida will call with a word of his own, *the conversion*).[37] And how can one resist its charm. And the stupefying inner adventure of the subject Freud to which it leads us? I can't not take it. However, I'd like to tell you (I warn you) that you won't find our ladder in the German text, or in the English text either. Do I have to pull the ladder, for the reason that it will have been deployed by translation? But who knows – and I must mention such a hypothesis here – if there has not been thought transmission in this case, and if Freud did not suggest to the female translator that she should provide him with a ladder just when needed? The day when, in spite of the entreaties of his entourage, he gets ready to pass into the *enchanted* territory of the fairy Tarapatapoum Telepathy? Talking of translation,

51

that is to say, of deferred thought transmission: I wish I had the time here to invite you to a mental feast [*banquet*]. I would have suggested that you savour all the versions that came to my knowledge of this moment which is so important in the path of our hero. You would taste many a surprise. Each lecture, new and false, indeed falsifies the one adjacent to it, in fireworks galore [*à gogo*]. I will only cite one example here. Let's take this forceful, sober sentence which will be the driving force behind Freud's psychical or teleanalytic revolution. In French Freud supposedly said this:

Par le phénomène télépathique, l'acte psychique accompli par une certaine personne doit provoquer la réalisation d'un acte semblable chez une autre. Ce qui se produit entre deux actes psychiques peut facilement être un phénomène physique à point de départ et aboutissant psychiques. L'analogie avec d'autres transpositions, telles, par exemple, que l'émission et l'audition au téléphone, serait alors indiscutable.[38]

When communication takes place via the English language:

The telepathic process is supposed to consist in a mental act in one person instigating the same mental act in another person.[39]

Whereas Freud himself wrote:

Der telepathische Vorgang soll ja darin bestehen, daß ein seelischer Akt der einen Person den nämlichen seelischen Akt bei einer anderen Person anregt. Was zwischen den beiden

seelichen Akten liegt, kann leicht ein physikalischer Vorgang
sein, in den sich das Psychische an einem Ende umsetzt und
der sich am anderen Ende wieder in das gleiche Psychische
umsetzt.[40]

We won't have forgotten the event which comes hardly a page before these lines, but what a page! One would almost think it is a tall portal which had always been stubbornly closed to the other world, and this, as you can witness, even though Freud had been trying to get in for more than ten years. And lo and behold it opens from one moment to the next. In three words belief has been totally changed. As follows: '*Ich denke heute anders.*' Until the day before I was thinking in such and such a direction. 'To-day I think otherwise.' This is an extraordinary, unique thought event. And one which did not take place, except in a dream. One should not forget that Freud did not utter this formula of recantation, of conjuration, of confession, of revelation. Except to himself. This declaration will therefore have remained unvoiced and inaudible.

'To-day I think otherwise,'[41] he said. A to-day which will not have taken place, except in a book. Those who will later echo this reversal will be able to indulge in a few adjustments. After all Freud never said that. He only *wrote* these texts, which therefore have the same force of faked truth, neither more nor less, as a literary work. The very words of this Freud who went down the road of imagination, for instance the word *seelisch, the word of the soul,* will be brought back to reason by keeping the appearance of fairness, and by taking advantage of the fact that some languages prefer to use the word mind/

53

spirit or the 'psychic' word, from *psukhé*, for the Latin word *anima*.

Seelisch will therefore not be deemed relevant [*relevé*] in translation. Nor this very particular moment when Freud has crossed in his imagination the gates which run alongside and enclose the banks of the Lethe. In forgotten times, says the Germanic legend, it was believed that the *Seelen* of beings lived before birth and after death, under the water of a *See*, a sea or a lake.

– There you go, you will say (writes Freud, who pretends to read in the thoughts of his imaginary disciples), the old man is lapsing into second childhood. We know that. 'Yet again we are dealing with a man who has studied honestly the sciences of Nature all his life and who, with the onset of old age, becomes weak of mind, pious and credulous.'[42] In short: gaga. But it is not the case. On the contrary, I hoisted myself up on the ladder, and I went back to the child in me who could see the invisible and who has forgotten nothing.

How many times over ten years, my friends, my dear Jones, you have seen me thus, during a walk, stop in front of an avenue opening out in front of us, or in front of a clump of trees, ask you to leave me alone for a moment, said Freud in writing, while expressing in a strange way but in German the same covert complaint as the one Proust on his side modulated in a similar way but in French. As if the two secretly inspired [*inspirés au secret*] were standing unknowingly at the same time at both ends of rue de la Pompe. Both of them. Each of them separately [*de son côté*]. Is traversed by the thought of another who, younger and more aggressive, and who is also himself annoyed by the lack of imagination of his next of kin, exclaims: the unconscious, here's one of those things 'between heaven and earth which philosophy refuses to dream of'.[43]

Meanwhile, on my side, I witness as in a dream this meeting of geniuses trembling in front of the infinites, I hasten to note the features of this experience of reality: each time the illuminative event takes place during *a walk*. One needs trees. Behind the curtain *one cannot see the sea*. This not-to-see is also a telepathic act.

I can see you looking at me looking, eyes afar, at what is situated only at a soul's distance. A *soul's distance* is how we, the mystical freemasonry, name in private what I learnedly call *telepathy* when I discourse in public and resume my rank and talk among my suspicious friends

In the corner of my dream, I keep: *âme* (soul); and also *d'âme* –

You think I cannot hear you think? You're saying to yourself in a whisper: now Doctor Freud is losing his head. One must not say that. Well, I am saying it to you today, if you want to go further on the narrow path which leads to discovery, you must lose your head, yes, there's a head which must be lost, the head that knows, that is to say, that thinks it knows, too fast, the one Proust denounces and runs away from, this *intelligence* head which prevents the sensation from finding its name and the trees with arms stretched out entreatingly from resurrecting. For it is the ones who *believe* they know who are truly credulous, the believers, the arrived, the immobile. Whereas those who are on a walk and do not know, and are tempted by the sirens of oblivion and of memory, and scrutinize the piece of green curtain hung in front of the broken glass screen, wondering what is happening to them, those come near the point of

55

apocalypse. An intoxication whispers to them it is going to take place, it is going to take place... The times are near. As follows: the prisons crumble. The gates throw their bars wide open.

At that moment 'the people' of the book, as Proust calls them, for the people, *gens*, are all virtual *Jean* by homophony, aren't they, divide into two parties, or parts. Some do not go further, do not want to or cannot Go go.[44] They do not take the step. – *I am stumped*, says one of them. I recognize the voice of Jacques Derrida. – I cannot see anything any more. In vain I look round the square of green canvas for the places, says another one, anxious about turning his back to the dead who were hoping to return [*revenir*]. But for the others, those of Gogo's party, the surprise that lies in store for them round the corner with its golden cart is *the first Communion*. Its most detailed and most deeply moving account can be found at the beginning of the fourth part of *Peter Ibbetson*. I'll only give a paltry summary of it here. You will see how our overwhelmed hero has a dream. In the dream he walks near the gate on the avenue. Instead of the school there is a prison. He's going to be thrown there and hanged. Mad with terror, he rushes towards the gate on the avenue. There he finds the Duchess of Towers. It is a divine vision of reality. – What you're dreaming here is not true, she says in the dream. Give me your hand and come in here. In the true dream, at the contact of her hand, he senses he is no longer in the horrible, deceptive dream. The weirdest thing in the world happens to him: a new life. This new life takes place in a dream but in a true dream. In this true dream he does know who he is, he knows he does sleep in his bed on the fourth floor of the hotel, he pinches himself to make sure he is fully awake, and he is. And yet he finds himself holding hands with a *grande d'âme*, a great lady with a great soul to whom he has never been introduced and who is smiling at him. He is therefore truly dreamt. Awake. The Dream is there. All this is such a wonderful dreamery [*rêvier*].

I was still holding the duchess's hand, and felt the warmth of it through her glove; it stole up my arm like a magnetic current. I was in Elysium; a heavenly sense had come over me that at last my periphery had been victoriously invaded by a spirit other than mine – a most powerful and beneficent spirit. There was a blessed fault in my impenetrable armor of self, after all, and the genius of strength and charity and loving-kindness had found it out.

'Now you're dreaming true,' she said. 'Where are those boys going?'

'To church, to make their *première communion*,' I replied.

'That's right. You're dreaming true because I've got you by the hand. Do you know that tune?'

I listened, and the words belonging to it came out of the past and I said them to her, and she laughed again, with her eyes screwed up deliciously.

'Quite right – quite!' she exclaimed. 'How odd that you should know them! How well you pronounce French for an Englishman! For you are Mr Ibbetson, Lady Cray's architect?'[45]

What an enchantment!

Perhaps he is dead? Thus to sleep, perchance to dream[46] – that's how it is.

The gate, the same gate, but painted in a dream.

She asks him to read the inscription in letters of gold on the portico of the house of his childhood. He deciphers: Parvis Notre-Dame. It is therefore a dream indeed. In reality he would have read *Parva sed Apta*. But it is reality indeed since he is in front of the Lady [*Dame*] whence his life, and light, starts. At second glance he correctly reads *Parva sed Apta*. For the dream has a sense of the true like the *Dame d'âme*. Now the Duchess of Towers, whom he has seen only from a distance before, teaches him with extreme care how to dream true. Everything is difficult and everything is easy. You must join the dream on to reality and not cease for a single moment being fully awake in the dream. 'Ce n'est que le premier pas qui coûte,'[47] she says. Her voice emphasizes these words.

Regretfully, with the anguish one feels when one reluctantly betrays the living and the dead, I interrupt here, constrained by time's brevity, the account of this true dream of which these paltry lines represent a mere hundredth. You should know that the divine walk of Peter Ibbetson soon followed or preceded by Gogo Pasquier will have led us via all the caves of the earth and on all the seas of the sky, in the joined kingdoms, until the following sentence: 'Do speak English, Mimsey, please.'

A little girl ran up the avenue from the porter's lodge and pushed the garden gate, which rang the bell as it opened, and she went into the garden, and I followed her; but she took no notice of me, nor did the others. It was Mimsey Seraskier.

[. . .] Mimsey said –

'Regarde Médor, comme il remue la queue! *C'est le Prince Charmant qui lui chatouille le bout du nez.*'

Said my mother, who had not spoken hitherto: 'Do speak English, Mimsey, please.'

Oh, my God! My mother's voice, so forgotten, yet so familiar, so unutterably dear! I rushed to her, and threw myself on my knees at her feet, and seized her hand and kissed it, crying, 'Mother, mother!'

A strange blur came over everything; the sense of reality was lost. All became as a dream – a beautiful dream – but only a dream; and I woke.[48]

– Only the first step is costly.

– *No, for us every step is costly*, says Jacques Derrida.

– Freud says that in French, notes Jacques Derrida in his duel with the forger of the *New Lectures*. The duel of two blind men who are trying to make each other lose their heads and occasionally swap each other's thoughts, pinch them, shake them from within. And, says Jacques Derrida, 'he concludes: *das weitere findet sich*'. That is in German. As if something were thinking in two languages in Freud's head, as if he were talking to himself from a distance, under the influence of an intense inner autotelepathy. I reread Jacques Derrida. He is very cross, actually. Admittedly his furious words are supposed to be privately reserved for the recipient of these fake letters, hence the dishevelled tone of his resentment:

Having had the cheek to say that his life has been very poor in terms of occult experiences, he adds: but what a step beyond it would be if . . . (*welch folgenschwerer Schritt über. . .*). So he envisages the consequences and adds the story of the guardian of the Saint-Denis basilica. Saint Denis had walked with his head under his arm after his beheading. He had walked a fair distance (*ein ganzes Stück*). And you know what he had done with his head, to put it under his arm? He had lifted it up [*relevée; aufgehoben*].⁴⁹

True, it can be said that, as a false Freud, Jacques Derrida will have really taken us not for a walk but for a ride [*se sera bien payé notre tête*] with his act as an acrobat puppeteer who plays all antagonistic roles, tumbles himself, worms secrets out of himself for himself [*se tire les vers du nez de l'autre nez*], puts his Freud's head on the block that he himself does not know if he knows if he believes or if he does not believe himself

And why does the Duchess of Towers say that *c'est le premier pas qui coûte* in French?

'On revient toujours à ses premières amours' (one always returns to one's first loves). Freud says that too in French. It is the voice of the inner stranger, who talks to him about himself, the one he was the one he no longer is but in a dream.

The first Duchess of Towers returns, it's the thirteenth time and it is still the first, I still love for the first time, the thirteenth first time, the same giant lean soft Tower which is half a head taller than my mother and who is my mother even when lost, my mother who grows with my sorrow and my desire. Contrary to common observation, the loved object grows with distance. There is a narrow relation between the Towers of the Soul [*Tours d'Âme*] and prison.

I return. It does not happen deliberately. We are transported by a fortuitous chance. A piece of green canvas stops us short. There is a hole in the pane. It is enough to make the step by slipping or telepathing on all fours and eight paws [*à quatre pattes ou huit, à quatre pathies*], in order to find oneself back at the starting point of the path of Revelations.

ONOMATELEPATHY

I am writing all this telepathically with Aletheia my magic cat. She mimes everything I think at the very moment. While with a beating heart I sink deeper into the sublime path leading to the Dreaming True, I can see her truedreaming with a beating heart and quivering nostrils by my side, she never stopped looking at me in the eyes I was still holding the hand, she was squeezing my hand in hers, and felt the warmth of it through her white fur glove. We were in the same dream. It stole up my arm like a magnetic current. I was in Elysium.[50] 'I felt uneasy, smelt odours of geraniums and orange trees, felt a sensation of extraordinary light and of happiness.'[51] This sentence was by Proust, this sensation was mine, I could see the message from these eternal bygone days with pink nostrils speckled with Aletheia's moles rising, the sentence too was rolling along her slender spine, I was writing, I was reading, I was walking along rue du Cercle Militaire simultaneously, with sentences singing by my side, colours of geraniums and orange trees by Aletheia's sides, an extraordinarily tall gate thrust up its stiff spears in front of me. We were in Oran, at the starting point. The light from the felicitous past has a clarity which no actual incident can pollute. *O the pure life kept pure.*[52] And never has *the Gate* been so monumental and authoritarian. I recognized it for what it had always been and would be until the end: the sign of my destiny. The Gate. The Portal. The bars. And all the distance and separation from the world, which cannot be measured in kilometres, in the narrow, inflexible thickness of those bars. Am I inside? Am I outside?

And my trees! My slim, elegant acacias, my first loves, my magnolias, my madly seducing mimosas, my half-loving half-words, they stretch out their arms to me, my arms, my trees, my young odorous orpheuses from Oran, always already powerless, I adore you, I said, and the Glass always already separates us, I can *see* them *telling* me *regretfully* that they cannot *tell* me the *secret*, their beautiful pursed lips sketch all the words, but the Pane [*Vitre*], the invisible transparent substance which cuts out the sound, thwarts our voices. Pains [*vitrifie*] our lives. We see ourselves/one another voiceless. It's torture. I want to enter. I must enter. I want to pass into the side of trees which stretch out to me the passionate, powerless arms of my father leaving us, which I stretched out, o powerful powerlessness, to my father while the distance resounded increasingly strongly between us. I look for the hole in the Pane. The passport for the portal. If I am not granted the right, I will turn myself into a cat, pass through the bars. Everything calls me. Words mock at me. The other day I ran to throw myself at the necks of trees I thought it was my father, the tree over there, thin, upright, and I crashed on to bars. How naïve and passionate we are in The Garden where, in its finest attire sewn with nasturtiums and convolvulus, girt with wisterias and jasmines, the Promised Prison awaits us, its Behemoth jaws gaping. Gardens guard. Themselves. Guard from guarding. I am the result of an adorable and absolutely impenetrable Garden which has initiated me into the mystery of *confinement* in paradise. No entry. Thou shalt not enter. I did not enter. We did not enter. One fine morning I entered the Magic Circle. The portal made way. I believed I entered. I believed I was inside. The Gates being cleared, I doubtless had to find myself inside. I did not find myself there. I was inside and I was not. It's a nightmare, I said to myself. I was fully awake and I was in a nightmare. No matter how objectively I was inside, I had never been so arrested, so much a stranger in the midst of a strange land, yet I felt mentally uneasy, odours of geraniums and orange trees were speaking to me, yet I was repelled, chased away, instead of my name another name, instead of Gogo Pasquier, Peter Ibbetson, instead of Hélène, Jewess. Instead of paths lined with trees so dear, forests of bars. I have already written all this.

A true nightmare is inexhaustible. It grows and multiplies. I could cite hundreds of dreams of confinement, I have repeated the same mistake of illusion a thousand times. I enter I believe I believe I reach the heart of things, I am at the bottom of the outside, one more time. But each time I look for the way out. How to exit fate [*sortir du sort*]? Outside is my fate. The voice of the Gates touches me, the mixture of odours of jail and orange tree intoxicates me and goes to my head.

I was two of us, locked in the impenetrable Circle, my brother was making the other philippine, two seeds in the same pod. He does not remember Hell. He has not forgotten. He was not yet born to memory it was before his language. Only I have the scar. But each time it opens its lips from a distance he has the same sensation, from one town to another we commune in the confinement outside. Why did I often find myself in a walk in which I indulge ecstatically, which enchants me and leads me in front of a curtain of bars? I cannot not respond to the invitation. Go![53] I go. It is the natural movement of my planet. Peter Ibbetson does not complain about the prison to which he is sentenced for life. It is a shell *Parva sed Apta*, tightly fitting, poor, from which he learnt how to make philippine with the Duchess of Towers. These telepathic walks took place in their country where it is bright all night long, till their last hour.[54]

Each time there's Prison, I pray, I do my utmost to change it into a garden. Each time I see myself thrilled/ ravished [*ravie*] in a garden, I fear lest it turn into a prison from one moment to the next. I watch out for the slightest signs. I watch over the ants. Let them not mutate into the military! The worst things can happen, bombings, witchcraft trials, diseases, if one does not pay attention to what lies hidden in the bushes. Everything is treacherous. The venomous powers (like the salvational powers) lie dormant everywhere, especially in words. One dream and they jump on the opportunity. Take, for example, Peter Ibbetson's lost hidden name, that is to say, Pierre de la Marier. It is so discreet, almost unknown. I never think about Pierre, nor about Marier, especially since he has another name, Pasquier, over which there is yet another. There's Pierre as well, my mother's son. Pete is what I call my brother. One loves the man, one loves what touches him, unknowingly. All of a sudden I am at Church. I myself feel slightly astonished about it. – And what are-*you*-doing-here? (I ask myself in a telepathic aside [*en apartélépathie*]).

– I have agreed to get married. – The horror! *I* did that? – I am in despair. It's done, I've done the deed, as they say. It's me there, in a white gown, with the priest, that old bloke in a red gown, who bows. *I* did this to myself?! What was I thinking about? The priest meanwhile says: 5000 francs.

– It is only the first false step [*faux pas*] that is costly, I thought. Not at all, says my mother. It's going to cost me 1.5 million. As soon as I start spending [*dépenser*], she wants a penny for my thoughts [*elle lit dans mes pensées*]. She begins to do the accounts. Oh! who will save me? I come round/return to myself [*reviens à moi*] all at once. Marry [*Marier*]? Me? – It's a mistake! A stroke of homophony. – And on top of that, my mother thinks sorrowfully, there'll be the divorce expenditure

Too late. It's a Freudian slip [*lapsus*]. I try to accept the verdict. Well. I'll soon see myself phoning Jacques Derrida. I can see him saying: what's new? Then I will be seen saying to him: you know, I got married today. I can hear my voice: it sounds perfectly natural. Unfortunately he does not hear. I say it again: I got married. This time it's a bit less of a success. In the meantime the word has swollen. – 'So, he says, what do you want me to say?'

Oh! Here I recognize the sentence – and I know what follows. It is the beginning of 'Telepathy', I quote 'I had a premonition of something nasty in it, like a word, or a worm [. . .].'[55] Yes he will say these words, these sentences. No, no, I won't phone. How shameful! It's useless: I can already hear what he will say. Let's return to the unacceptable reality. So I got married but it was in my absence. *I*, here and now proclaim it without shame, at the risk of causing a scandal in front of all the flabbergasted guests who walk alongside me on the small path which winds its way between the threshold of the Church – for the whole of this Church is nothing but a threshold – and the drawing room where I forgot to make preparations for the champagne, *I am against marriage. On principle.* Never marry. I therefore cannot want what happened to me. What can be done? Too bad for the money. I won't go into detail. If that priest had not been there. There was no husband anyway. That would take the biscuit. This undeniable statement remains, *je suis Marier*. Fortunately there occurs to me at that moment an idea as luminous and redemptive as the Duchess of Towers at the gate of avenue de la Pompe: At least I did not get married in the town hall! It was only a Church. This horrible moment has no *legal* value. Now I am out of this quandary [*tirée de ce faux pas*]. I'm going to be able to wake up. My interest is to prevent the Dream from taking advantage of my sleep so I don't find myself in the town hall. Up! The day is breaking, I write: I am not married. Not that I deny having been Marier. What had astonished me during the dream – not to have felt any sort of astonishment nor guilt – instantly caught light. At last I recognized the word, the truth. I was this Marier,

70

this forgotten Pierre, this visionary stroller whom love will have initiated into dreaming true. I recognize that, in the whole duration of the book, this Pierre was as dear to me as people in life, I made Philippine with him. We have been in the same *Mandorla*. I like this explanation better. I phone Jacques Derrida. As usual it is extremely early. I'm waking you up? I dreamt about you. He tells me his dream. According to him I had got married to my brother. He is not sure of that. He uses the word *remarier* (remarry). Maybe I was my brother eventually. All that was taking place in the Jardin d'Essai. By way of a Church, there was a tree whose name he has forgotten. So have I, I say. A charming tree, with flexible arms, with very fragrant, white flowers arranged in white clusters. I can see it very well. The entrance to the Cercle Militaire was scented with its fragrance. A kind of acacia, I say. But a false one. All is truefalse, he says. It's the same for telepathy. There is only hypotelepathy. It exists in a dream. If it exists in a dream it therefore exists in reality. If there is a telepathy in reality, which I will call an if-telepathy [*sitélépathie*],[56] then one can *vermuten*, he says, that despite the difficulty, not the impossibility, to prove it, it is a *recht häufiges Phänomen*. You're speaking in Francogerman now? I say. In Deutschfrançais, he says. It is the proof we are swimming in the imaginary and truly-real waters of Seelepathy. In those twilight zones where the demarcation lines are erased, where one changes one's body as one changes horses, where the town of one's birth resurrects at each step, one naturally indulges in amphibiology and bilingualism. Thus one overcomes the obstacles of time's portals. – You see the trees at the entrance to the Garden of the Cercle Militaire? I say to my brother. Outside? he says – Inside, I say. I can see them very well. An almond tree? A peppery scent reaches me. False acacias, I say. – You think so? – Smell, I say. I crumple the narrow leaves which cover it like feathers. It is the fragrance of the unforgettable.

One cannot give *proofs* of the dreamingtrue. Or of telepathy. Since it takes place inside in the inner foreign country.

Telepathy is a matter of habit, says Freud to himself. It remains to know how to get into it. It is the same for dreams. It is the same for cats. The more I listen to them, the more they speak to me. Their faithfulness depends on my faithfulness. The more I dream, the more I allow myself to dream/to be dreamt, the more dreams come to me. It is the same for the trees which stretch out their arms to us. Some of our friends don't want to hear a thing about it. They walk past an avenue which opens out and they do not take the path. Yet those so power-fully powerless arms, which only wait for a glance to cry out a name to call me, are mine, it is the little one – the child who was happy and who is the keeper of happiness in my ruins, who holds them out to me. Here's the gate. An avenue *goes*. The intense humming of insects and of light. Careful! Life is going to start again. Let's cross the bars. – Go! Go![57] One more step. The narrow path is going to lead us to the magnificent prospect. 'I feel I have in my mind like the lake invisible at night. . . But I feel that a mere nothing can break this brainshell. . . Hold your crown tight' . . .

NOTES

1 Marcel Proust, *Carnets*, ed. Florence Callu and Antoine Compagnon (Paris: Gallimard, 2002), p. 50. Followed by: 'I stare ahead at four maidens' heads and no longer see the reality which at present is uniformly forgotten> / But I feel that a mere nothing can break this brainshell. man of letters near Cabourg working in the hope of seeing friends from time to time, of ~~showing~~ seeming great to them through what he does, then the thought of his friends supersedes them, never sees them. Marcel goes to see him, without having read anything by him, piece on Harrison. Baldwin Stairs, Potocka, moments when one sees truthful reality with enthusiasm, stripped of habit, novelty, intoxication, memory. Whistling trains describing the countryside near the cliff at moonlight, in the cold night at Illiers, Versailles, St Germain, Sollier. Alighting from the train. Cobblestones trodden with

joy. Félicie's cobblestones glisten^g with moon. Dream in which Félicie says to me: it is because of your trional, thus dream composed by me in which she learns from me what she cannot know and in which however I am myself igno-rant, beautiful mosaic, with colours mingling ignorance and knowledge, mysterious truth only one sweet to my jaded eyes. / Chateaubriand and me realized sylph (see *Revue de Paris*, 15 September 1908, p. 379) ~~does not~~ yield to the temptation to' (pp. 50–1). (Trans. from the original by Laurent Milesi.)

2 Proust, *Mélanges*, in *Contre Sainte-Beuve; précédé de Pastiches et mélanges; et suivi de Essais et articles*, ed. Pierre Clarac with the collaboration of Yves Sandre (Paris: Gallimard, 1971), p. 801 (trans. from the original by Laurent Milesi).

3 This refers to the wild fig tree on the Palatine Hill in ancient Rome. The tree was said to be sacred to the god-dess Rumina and, according to tradition, is the spot where the trough containing Romulus and Remus landed on the banks of the Tiber and where they were reared by a she-wolf. – Trans.

4 Sigmund Freud, 'Vorwort', in *Vorlesungen zur Einführung in die Psychoanalyse und Neue Folge*, vol. 1 (Frankfurt am Main: S. Fischer, 2003), p. 449; *The Standard Edition of the Complete Psychological Works of Sigmund Freud*, vol. XXII (1932–1936): *New Introductory Lectures on Psycho-Analysis and Other Works*, trans. and gen. ed. James Strachey (London: Hogarth Press, 1964), p. 5.

5 Freud, *Vorlesungen zur Einführung in die Psychoanalyse und Neue Folge*, vol. 1, p. 496; *New Introductory Lectures*, in *The Standard Edition*, vol. XXII, p. 57.

6 *Faire faux bond*: to let somebody down; a shared Derridean and Cixous leitmotif. Cf. also n. 25 below – Trans.

7 George du Maurier, *Peter Ibbetson*, with an Introduction by His Cousin Lady **** (Madge Plunket), ed. George du Maurier (Charleston, SC: BiblioBazaar, 2006), p. 192.

8 In dated French slang, this also designates a female traffic warden (cf. *amende*: fine, above). – Trans.

9 Perhaps also French *monder*: to blanch (almonds). – Trans.

10 'PHILIPPINE: n. and a., a late introduction (1898), is the altered form, through attraction of the first name *Philippe*, of the German word *Vielliebchen*, "much loved", from *viel*, "much", and the diminutive of *lieb*, "loved", "dear". Like corresponding words *viel* rests on the neutral form of a Germanic adjective *felu-*, which is related to the Indo-European root of Greek *polu-* (whence "poly-"), having the same meaning. *Lieb* corresponds to archaic English *lief*, Dutch *lief*, Old Norse *ljúfr*, an adjective related to English "love". Its Indo-European base can be found in Latin *libet*, "it pleases me" (whence "libido") and Old Slavonic *ljubû*, "dear". *Vielliebchen* is used to designate a game played with double almonds [*amandes jumelles*] as well as, by extension, these almonds (bef. 1850). It is probably altered from English "valentine" (1450) or French *valentin*, *valentine*, having the same meaning, derived from the saint name *Valentin*. The meaning of "double almonds" (1839) and of "game" (1879) is also known in English.' Translated from *Le Robert. Dictionnaire historique de la langue française*, 3 vols (Paris: Robert, 2004).

11 Paul Celan, '*Die Niemandsrose*' (1961), in *Die Gedichte* (Frankfurt am Main: Suhrkamp, 2003), p. 142; *Poems of Paul Celan*, trans. and intr. Michael Hamburger, new edn (London: Anvil Press, 1995), pp. 156–7.

12 'You ask me to name "ten good books" for you [. . .] I will

75

therefore name ten such "good" books for you which have come to my mind without a great deal of reflection.

Multatuli, *Letters and Works*.

Kipling, *Jungle Book*.

Anatole France, *Sur la pierre blanche*.

Zola, *Fécondité*.

Merezhkovsky, *Leonardo da Vinci*.

G. Keller, *Leute von Seldwyla*.

C.F. Meyer, *Huttens letzte Tage*.

Macaulay, *Essays*.

Gomperz, *Griechische Denker*.

Mark Twain, *Sketches*.

I do not know what you intend to do with this list. It seems a most peculiar one even to me; I really cannot let it go without comment. The problem of why precisely these and not other equally "good" books I will not begin to tackle; I merely wish to throw light on the relation between the author and his work. The connection is not in every case as firm as it is, for instance, with Kipling's *Jungle Book*.' Freud, 'Contribution to a Questionnaire on Reading' (1907), in *The Standard Edition*, vol. IX (1906–1908): *Jensen's 'Gradiva' and Other Works* (London: Hogarth Press, 1959), pp. 245–6.

13 In English in the text. – Trans.

14 'For when an author makes the characters constructed by his imagination dream, he follows the everyday experience that people's thoughts and feelings are continued in sleep and he aims at nothing else than to depict his heroes' states of mind by their dreams. But creative writers are valuable allies and their evidence is to be prized highly, for they are apt to know a whole host of things between heaven and earth of which our philosophy has

not yet let us dream. In their knowledge of the mind they are far in advance of us everyday people, for they draw upon sources which we have not yet opened up for science.' Freud, 'Jensen's *Gradiva*' (1907), in *The Standard Edition*, vol. IX, p. 8.

15 In English in the text. – Trans.

16 In French the actor's family name sounds like '*coups père*', hence what follows (lit.: the father any time). – Trans.

17 Proust, 'Notes sur la littérature et la critique', in *Contre Sainte-Beuve*, p. 303 (trans. from the original by Laurent Milesi).

18 A famous retort in Jean de La Fontaine's fable of 'The Wolf and the Lamb'. – Trans.

19 In English in the text. – Trans.

20 Meaning 'son of' in Arabic names. – Trans.

21 '*la Manche sait se taire*', a hilarious pun sounding like Manchester. – Trans.

22 In English in the text. – Trans.

23 Du Maurier, *Peter Ibbetson*, pp. 45–6.

24 'On one side of the beautiful garden was another beautiful garden, separated from ours by a high wall covered with peach and pear and plum and apricot trees; on the other, accessible to us through a small door in another lower wall clothed with jasmine, clematis, convolvulus, and nasturtium, was a long, straight avenue of almond-trees, acacia, laburnum, lilac, and may, so closely planted that the ivy-grown walls on either side could scarcely be seen. What lovely patches they made on the ground when the sun shone! One end of this abutted on "the Street of the Pump," from which it was fenced by tall, elaborately-carved iron gates between stone portals, [. . .]

The other end of the avenue, where there was also an

iron gate, admitted to a large private park that seemed to belong to nobody, and of which we were free – a very wilderness of delight, a heaven, a terror of tangled thickets and not too dangerous chalk cliffs, disused old quarries and dark caverns, prairies of lush grass, sedgy pools, turnip fields, forests of pine, groves and avenues of horse-chestnut, dank valleys of walnut-trees and hawthorn, which summer made dark at noon; bare, wind-swept mountainous regions whence one could reconnoitre afar; all sorts of wild and fearsome places for savages and wild beasts to hide and small boys to roam quite safely in quest of perilous adventure.

[. . .] an Eden where one might gather and eat of the fruit of the tree of knowledge without fear, and learn lovingly the ways of life without losing one's innocence; a forest that had remade for itself a new virginity, and become primeval once more; where beautiful Nature had reasserted her own sweet will, and massed and tangled everything together as though a Beauty had been sleeping there undisturbed for close on a hundred years, and was only waiting for the charming Prince.' Du Maurier, *Peter Ibbetson*, pp. 16–17.

25 (*il ne*) *faut pas* signals something forbidden; *faux* and *faut* are homophones in French. – Trans.

26 Jacques Derrida, 'Telepathy', trans. Nicholas Royle, in *Psyche: Inventions of the Other*, vol. I, ed. Peggy Kamuf and Elizabeth Rottenberg (Stanford: Stanford University Press, 2007), p. 234.

27 In English in the text: a reference to *Hamlet*, I.v.152, followed in the original by a French equivalent. – Trans.

28 *Dutikos*: who enjoys diving, like the Dioscorides. From *duein*: to plunge, to dive.

29 Proust, *Après la guerre*, Préface, in *Contre Sainte-Beuve*, p. 571 (trans. from the original by Laurent Milesi).

30 An allusion to *pompes funèbres*: undertakers, funeral directors. – Trans.

31 'A prefatory note to the German edition states that the paper "was written for the meeting of the central Executive of the International Psycho-Analytical Association held in the Harz mountains at the beginning of September, 1921." Dr Ernest Jones, who was at the time President of the Central Executive, tells us, however, that no meeting of that body took place in the Harz mountains at the date in question, though there was a gathering of Freud's closest followers: Abraham, Eittingon, Ferenczi, Rank and Sachs, besides Dr Jones himself. It was to this unofficial group that the paper seems to have been read.

Freud had intended the paper to give reports of three cases, but when he came to prepare the MS, at Gastein he found that he had left the material for the third case behind in Vienna, and he was obliged to replace it by some material of a rather different character.' 'Psycho-Analysis and Telepathy' (1921), in *The Standard Edition*, vol. XVIII (1920–1922): *Beyond the Pleasure Principle, Group Psychology and Other Works*, p. 175. [Note in English in the text. – Trans.]

32 '*Also hören Sie: An einem Herbsttag des Jahres 1919, etwa um ¾ 11 Uhr a. m., gibt der eben aus London eingetroffene Dr David Forsytheine Karte für mich ab, während ich mit einem Patienten arbeite. (Mein geehrter Kollege von der London University wird es sicherlich nicht als Indiskretion auffassen, wenn ich so verrate, daß er sich von mir durch einige Monate in der Künste der psychoanalytischen Technik einführen ließ.) Ich habe nur Zeit, ihn zu begrüssen und für später zu bestellen.*'

Freud, *Vorlesungen zur Einführung in die Psychoanalyse und Neue Folge*, vol. I, p. 51. [Note in German in the text. – Trans.]

33 Also in English in the text. – Trans.

34 Here Cixous's note refers to the Kessinger Publishing edition of *Peter Ibbetson* in English, pp. 86–8, as support for the analogy between true (in English in the text) and *tour*. – Trans.

35 Du Maurier, *Peter Ibbetson*, p. 122. [The second excerpt comes first in the novel. – Trans.]

36 Derrida, 'Telepathy', p. 26: 'there is only tele-analysis [. . .]'.

37 This was followed by a page reference to the French version of 'Dreams and Occultism' in *New Introductory Lectures to Psychoanalysis*. – Trans.

38 Freud, 'Rêve et occultisme', *Nouvelles Conférences sur la psychanalyse*, trans. Anne Berman (Paris: Gallimard, 1936), p. 75.

39 Freud, 'Dreams and Occultism' (1933), in *The Standard Edition*, vol. XXII, p. 55.

40 Freud, 'Traum und Okkultismus', *Vorlesungen zur Einführung in die Psychoanalyse und Neue Folge*, vol. I, p. 493.

41 In English in the text. – Trans.

42 'I am aware that a few great names must be included in this class, but you should not reckon me among them. At least I have not become pious, and I hope not credulous. It is only that, if one has gone about all one's life bending in order to avoid a painful collision with the facts, so too in one's old age one still keeps one's back ready to bow before new realities. No doubt you would like me to hold fast to a moderate theism and show myself

relentless in my rejection of everything occult. But I am incapable of currying favour and I must urge you to have kindlier thoughts on the objective possibility of thought-transference and at the same time of telepathy as well.' Freud, 'Dreams and Occultism', in *The Standard Edition*, vol. XXII, p. 54.

43 Freud, 'Psycho-Analysis and Telepathy' (1921), in *The Standard Edition*, vol. XVIII, p. 178. [In English in the text. – Trans.]

44 In English in the text. – Trans.

45 Du Maurier, *Peter Ibbetson*, p. 120.

46 Echoes Hamlet's line in his famous 'To be or not to be' soliloquy, in *Hamlet* III.i.65. – Trans.

47 I.e. it's only the first step which is costly. This sentence is left in French; see Du Maurier, *Peter Ibbetson*, p. 131. Through some telepathic textual effect the phrase also appears in French in Freud's 'Psycho-Analysis and Telepathy'; see Derrida, 'Telepathy', p. 243. – Trans.

48 Du Maurier, *Peter Ibbetson*, pp. 124–5.

49 Derrida, 'Telepathy', p. 243.

50 Echoes the beginning of the quotation p. 50 above. – Trans.

51 Proust, *Contre Sainte-Beuve*, p. 212 (trans. from the original by Laurent Milesi).

52 Proust, *Contre Sainte-Beuve*, p. 212. – Trans.

53 In English in the text. – Trans.

54 'That night I had such an extraordinary dream! I dreamed I was floundering about the Rue de la Pompe, and had just got to the avenue gate, and you were there.' [. . .]
I. 'Yes; and there was a crowd [. . .] And an organ was playing a tune I knew quite well, but cannot now recall.'...
She. 'Wasn't it "Maman, les p'tits bateaux?"'

I. Oh, of *course!*

' "*Maman, les p'tits bateaux*
Qui vont sur l'eau,
Ont-ils des jambes?" '

She. 'That's it!'

' "*Eh oui, petit bêta!*
S'ils n'avaient pas
Ils n'march'raient pas!" '

She sank back in her chair, pale and prostrate. After a while –

She. 'And then I gave you good advice about how to dream true, and we got to my old house, and I tried to make you read the letters on the portico, and you read them wrong, and I laughed.' [. . .]

She. 'And then I touched you again and you read ' "Parvis Notre Dame." '

I. 'Yes! and you touched me *again*, and I read "Parva sed Apta" – small but fit.' [. . .]

I. [. . .] 'After this you gave me good advice again, about not touching anything or picking flowers. I never have. And then you went away into the park – the light went out of my life, sleeping or waking. I have never been able to dream of you since.' Du Maurier, *Peter Ibbetson*, pp. 140–2.

55 Derrida, 'Telepathy', p. 226.

56 '*Wenn es eine Telepathie als realen Vorgang gibt, so kann man trotz ihrer schweren Erweisbarkeit vermuten, daß sie ein recht häufiges Phänomen ist.*' Freud, 'Traum und Okkultismus', *Vorlesungen zur Einführung in die Psychoanalyse und Neue Folge*, vol. I, p. 60. [Note in German in the text. – Trans.]

57 In English in the text. – Trans.